T0374270

OTHER RELEVANT BOOKS

On the Trail of Artificial Intelligence

Advanced Lessons in Artificial Intelligence

Conspectus of Artificial Intelligence

Management of Artificial Intelligence

THE
K-REPORT

A NEW HYBRID WRITING GENRE

HARRY KATZAN JR.

THE K-REPORT
A NEW HYBRID WRITING GENRE

iUniverse books may be ordered through booksellers or by contacting:

iUniverse
1663 Liberty Drive
Bloomington, IN 47403
www.iuniverse.com
844-349-9409

Because of the dynamic nature of the Internet, any web addresses or links contained in this book may have changed since publication and may no longer be valid. The views expressed in this work are solely those of the author and do not necessarily reflect the views of the publisher, and the publisher hereby disclaims any responsibility for them.

Any people depicted in stock imagery provided by Getty Images are models, and such images are being used for illustrative purposes only. Certain stock imagery © Getty Images.

ISBN: 978-1-6632-6498-5 (sc)
ISBN: 978-1-6632-6500-5 (hc)
ISBN: 978-1-6632-6499-2 (e)

Library of Congress Control Number: 2024914498

Print information available on the last page.

iUniverse rev. date: 07/24/2024

For Margaret Now and Forever
With Love and Affection

CONTENTS

INTRODUCTION

Welcome to the K-Report. It is a method that will make your life better. That is, if you have to write something like a paper, book, term paper, essay, or anything else in that category. The first thing that will pop in to your mind is that it is AI, and we all know by now that the letters stand for Artificial Intelligence. The subject of this book uses AI, but it isn't AI.

The name Artificial Intelligence emanated from an academic conference at Dartmouth College in the summer of 1956. There is no great advantage at this time to mention the participants, except that they are all famous and extremely intelligence. It is proper, however, to mention that Claude Shannon and John McCarthy coined the catchy name Artificial Intelligence and a couple of other participants from Carnegie Tech – now Carnegie Mellon - namely Herbert Simon and Allen Newell coined the name Complex Information Processing. The zippy title Artificial Intelligence was selected, and one can imagine what it would be like today if the second title had won out.

Many persons, to this day, regard artificial intelligence to be a computer application that would require intelligence if done by a human person. One good definition for AI is "The ability to act in subtle ways when presented with a class of situations that have been exhaustively analyzed in advance, but which require different combinations of responses if the result in many specific cases is to be acceptable." This definition in various ways has been used by many people. The author,

Richard Hamming, is rarely mentioned. Through the normal academic process, many ideas become concepts. Such is the way that the intellectual system works. Most papers, novels, technical books, and academic textbooks use the result of other people's work.

One of the most useful concepts imbedded in AI is generative AI. Generative AI is a process that uses three forms: a foundation of information, an application model, and a sophisticated front end that makes the information useful. It is s a system that generates information for use by the end user.

With generative AI, a computer system is trained with reinforcement learning through human feedback, and a reward system that analyzes, combines various forms, and ranks the responses.

There is one well known generative AI product and it is known as ChatGPT, that processes text, next words, sentences, and paragraphs bases on some learning foundation. GPT is an acronym for Generative Pre-Trained Transformer and Chat is a bot that talks – in a sense and comes from Chatbot.

Human intellectual formulation is based on a generative model. You do not need to know this but it sounds good.

The notion of a K-Report is a hybrid writing form that combines the written word and generated information through a generative AI application. Through this process, much like human formulation, precise writing is accomplished with the combination of a written document and generated information.

This book is an example for the reader of a hypothetical problem that is addressed through human cooperation with generated information. The K-Report process helps to make a written contribution more exact and more efficient. The book itself relates a typical human problem with generated information. The example has no obvious application other than to inform the reader.

The Author
July, 2024

CHAPTER 1

ANOTHER CALL FROM THE WHITE HOUSE

Matt and Ashley were awakened by the usual 6 am call, but it was only 5:30. It was a call from the General, as usual, but he was not his normally calm self. He sounded a bit agitated.

"Can you be ready for a trip to Washington, at about 8 AM from our local airport?' asked the General.

"If you can be ready, we can be ready," said Matt. "However, we might be interested in where we are going, and what will we be doing when we get there. To start off, I personally would like to know if it is Washington or Langley, and should we pack for an overnight, or return tonight?"

"I do not know," said the General. "I am responding to a taped message. I will prepare for one overnight. It did not tell me to wear my dress uniform. I am a General for life, and I have to wear it as required. I am not going to wear it on this case."

"Who sent the message?" asked Matt.

"The White House, office of the President, and that's it," answered the General. "Mark Clark, director of Intelligence, was supposed to have retired, but I have received no information from hm on that subject. He's the one that usually calls me when our services are required. Maybe he hasn't retired. They do things like that when they can't find a suitable replacement.

I heard they are going to make a big change in intelligence, as a result of all the recent excitement over artificial intelligence."

"Maybe the new President is concerned over something – or should I say nervous?" said Matt.

"I'll try to call Clark," said the General. "I haven't heard from him since we were last involved with those guys."

"It's only been a week," said Matt. "Is Ashley going to be involved?"

"The message did not mention personnel, either you or Ashley. However, they know full well that if they want me, it involves the two of you."

"Thanks for the complement, Sir."

"I'm going to wear a dark suit and Ashley will do the equivalent," continued Matt. "Can you pick us up at 7:45?"

"I'll be there," replied the General. "Over and out. I haven't heard that is a few years."

<hr>

The general picked up Matt and Ashley, as planned, and they arrived at the commercial side of the airport at 7:55. The electric plane was waiting. Matt and Ashley each carried a small brief case with room for an overnight, and the General had a small rucksack. He was not in his dress uniform, because was not told to do so.

The group entered the slick new aircraft and the entry door to the electric plane closed automatically; the announcement mentioned that the aircraft was electric and they would proceed accordingly. The destination was Langley Virginia and the jurisdiction for the flight was the Intelligence Directorate. The flight proceeded without delay and was smooth and quick. After the flight ended, the general, Matt, and Ashley were met by an electric golf cart, and they were delivered forthwith to the director's conference room.

The General, Matt, and Ashley were escorted to their seats without introduction of any kind. The President stood up immediately and began to speak. The team looked at each other with amazement. The President did not use or need a microphone.

"Good morning, ladies, gentlemen, and military personal."

"I wonder what the military are," whispered Ashley to Matt.

Matt smiled and gave her a light elbow. The President smiled also but kept going.

"We are here to welcome the new Director of Intelligence, but at the last minute he changed his mind, because it would require that he resign from the Marine Corp. He is General William 'Bud' Lewis. To me, he is Bud as he is to his wife Kathryn, sitting in the audience. He will, however, assist us throughout the project. We have called former General Mark Clark back to the position as the Director of Intelligence, and he graciously agreed. So, he did not actually resign as anticipated. Bud is stationed as the military attaché in Russia, and will be returning to Russia after this meeting. He will be assisting us as the project progresses. Mr. Clark will continue with this meeting, as I am meeting with the 27 heads of US government offices on the subject of Artificial Intelligence. We have assigned a Director of Artificial Intelligence position to each of the aforementioned offices.

If I leave right now, I can make the scheduled meeting on time. Thanks for attending. Mr. Clark is in charge. *Godspeed!*"

———————»-◊-«———————

"Now, we know," said Clark as he talked to the audience. "I did not know of all of this until this morning. Bud and Kathryn, your plane back to Russia is waiting. I know you have been up until 5 o'clock this morning, so try to relax. As to the other people, please go back to your jobs; nothing has changed. To the General, Matt, and Ashley, it would appear that you were summoned on a wild goose chase. Please hang on. We will meet afterwards in my old office that is now my new office."

CHAPTER 2

MEETING WITH THE DIRECTOR

Ten minutes later, Director Clark, the General, Matt, and Ashley settled down in Clark's executive style office on the third floor.

"Coffee, anyone?" asked Mark Clark, the old/new Director of Intelligence in his old/new office.

"We haven't had a chance to have breakfast," said the General. "How about a little food?"

"My executive secretary thought of that," replied Clark. "It's in a secure room off the main of the main cafeteria."

Ten more minutes later, an awfully good looking breakfast of pancakes, scrambled eggs, and coffee was served. No one said a word until Ashley broke the eating, "These are the best scrambled eggs I have ever tasted; thanks."

"I'm really sorry for the confusion," said Clark. "This whole operation was thought up by the White House and the State Department. They both seem to be unusually worried about the Artificial Intelligence movement, and would like the Russians and the Chinese to believe the same way. The Intelligence Service is not at all worried because we are spending a proverbial fortune supporting university and commercial research and we are keeping track of it all. In the Intelligence Directory, we have a ChapGPT team, a neural network team, a deep learning team, and who knows what. Nevertheless, the President and the State Department want to have more evidence that we are leading the pack, even though we really do know the direction in which all of this is heading. They are even concerned that there might be an obscure US agency doing important research that gets inadvertently diverted to the Russians or Chinese. They are also concerned that other governments and their people can possible know better how to use Artificial Intelligence facilities than we know about and don't know how to use. So, there we go. It's our new job."

"How long will the project run?" asked Matt. "We have to make sure we don't stop too soon. We should try to find out how the new techniques evolve. What are the markers."

"We have a line in the President's secret budget that will run continuously until we overtly stop it," said Clark. "That may never happen. We do not use zero-base budgeting so line items run until they are purposely ended."

"I know about that," said Ashley. "We are paying for software for computers that are not used anywhere."

"You have unlimited expenses," said Clark. "Each of you will earn one million per month plus unlimited expenses. The General will take care of this, as before."

'You have to provide a progress report every month," continued Clark. "One more thing. Bud Lewis is on the team. He is our liaison and source in Russia. You can use him as required. He and his wife should be compensated as members of he team, even though they will be in Russia.

"When do we start?" asked the General.

"You just started, if you agree to be engaged in this project," said Clark. "You can pursue your academic careers as before. There should be no changes in that regard. People in our own government may be looking at you. I would like you to stay the night in our facility and give us a perspective on the subject tomorrow. Then you are on your own. Payment will be by direct deposit with no tax as before. You will have electric airplane service home as you got here. Thank you. I have been up so long that I can't remember when I last slept. Thank you for your service. Have a good day and evening."

CHAPTER 3

THE FIRST NIGHT IN INTELLIGENCE HEADQUARTERS

Matt and Ashley were escorted to their room and the General to his in the Langley facility. They agreed on the need to relax for a few hours and then meet in the larger of the rooms. They asked for some office supplies that were delivered in about ten minutes. Ashley fell asleep in a chair in their room as did the General in his. Matt was charged up and sat down at a small desk and started writing. After about 45 minutes, he stood up and started to walk around the room. Ashley awakened.

"What's going on Matt?" asked Ashley. "You are all worked up about something. Maybe we can go for a walk."

"Can we walk around this place?" replied Matt.

"Just call and find out hubby," said Ashley. "I think you need a mother."

Matt pushed a blue button on the phone and a woman answered.

"Can I help you Sir," someone said.

"I am Matt Miller..."

"I know who you are Dr. Miller," she said.

" Can we walk around the building?" asked Matt.

"You can do what you like, Sir." the receptionist said. "You, Mrs. Miller, and the General can do whatever you please

9

in this facility. All of you have the highest level of security in the government, and you can do what you please. We have eating facilities, fitness center, and a library."

"Do you have a golf course?" asked Matt with a smile on his face.

"Yes we do Sir," was the reply. "It is just out of the west door to the building. It is a 9-hole course and all required equipment is available."

"Thank you very much," replied Matt.

"There you go," said Ashley. "Seek and you shall find. Can I play golf with you and the General?"

"Sure," replied Matt. "You are my favorite golfing partner, but please do not tell the General."

Matt hit the blue button again and asked for the General. After a little irritation, Matt got the General.

"Good afternoon," said Matt. "How was your nap?"

"Not bad," answered the General. "It was a comfortable chair, They bear no expense around here."

"A little golf?" asked Matt. "I invite you. Be there be square. We'll pick you up on the way out."

———————⊰•◦•⊱———————

At the 9-hole course, there was a small office and a huge number of sets of clubs of various sizes. Each consisted of a carrying bag, a driver, a 9-iron, and a putter. Each of the players selected a set and a golf cap under the sign *Please return the golf clubs. You may keep the cap.*

The threesome had a joyous time and played a second

round. They didn't keep score, and decided that was the way to play. They had a light dinner and retired to the larger room.

"Matt has been busy, Sir," said Ashley. "While we were napping, Matt has been busy writing like a wild demon. Perhaps he will share his work with us now."

"Sure," answered Matt. "That's why I scribbled it out as fast I could write and then entered them into my iPhone neatly We can print them when we get home. My idea was that we don't exactly know what we will be doing, I just thought this might be a way of getting a handle on the tasks that we might have to deal with."

"Let's hear them," said the General. "But, let's just listen and save our comments until we get a printed copy."

"Okay, here we go," said Matt. When they get printed, there will be a space between the items for comments. Please realize that I have no idea of what we are supposed to do, and these are my thoughts on the current situation."

The mission originates at the highest level of the U.S. government.

> *The implication is that the U.S. government is doing well, relatively speaking, but it could do better because some of its problems are inherent in the system itself.*

> *A specific example is that there is a general impression that the U.S. way is the best way. Maybe the only way.*

Examples are in the area of business, and it results in the notion the U.S. is the only country that knows all there is to know about design, development, engineering, production, sales, and support. This feeling is from Americans.

Americans are the only ones that have brains and others are necessarily not intelligent.

It is true that Americans have evolved well in the sense that smart people marry and have smart children, and so forth. This is not the necessarily the case worldwide. Just a thought.

Americans think they are the only nation that knows about international relations.

The U.S. is the only country that knows how to fight wars, even though the allies in World War II (e.g., Russia) did very well indeed.

The U.S. is totally hung up on human rights.

The U.S. is the only country that knows anything about Artificial Intelligence, medicine, vaccines, epidemics, food preparation, and alcoholic beverages.

There are two countries, e.g., England and the U.S., that think they know what is best and should run the show. Especially England, and they do not like Americans. They often regard the U.S. as the colonies.

Propaganda exists in all nations. It is part of a strategy.

Other countries blame the U.S. for every problem that exists in the wide world.

Many Americans have come from foreign countries. They are not bad. Their work ethic is more than satisfactory.

Other countries steal technology from the U.S., including medicine, agriculture, and banking. When a worldwide problem arises, they wait for the U.S. to solve it.

Many persons come to the U.S. for various reason, and then criticize the U.S. No one has asked them to come here.

Many persons from foreign think they know how to run the U.S. and do not know anything about the situation. The U.S. should do this and that. It is not their business.

Americans should be getting tired of this and say so.

Americans think they know everything. In many cases and subjects, they do.

People from other counties do stupid things and expect the U.S. to support and help them out. They start wars and all kinds of other stuff. I expand on this later.

Many foreigners bring their social customs with them, and refuse to change. They think the U.S. should change for them.

Many counties criticize the U.S. but don't like it when Americans criticize them.

Foreigners think that they know how Americans should think and operate, when they do not understand the issues .

The U.S. supports most of the international organizations. Foreign countries expect help but do not pay their share.

The U.S. gives a lot of foreign aid and get nothing in return, except big trouble.

American should be careful with outsourcing to some foreign countries.

Foreigners should not be allowed to purchase U.S. assets, like China in the Midwest.

Foreigners should not be allowed to fly American airplanes, when they can't read the manuals. Also, some are two stupid to fly American planes.

Airplanes have exit doors in case of accidents. Airlines eliminate those doors to gain two or three seats. Foreign outsourcers do not understand this form of American stupidity when it exists. They do not understand American so-called logic that the customer gets what they want, even though it might not be the best of ideas.

Every mechanical device from washing machines to airplanes have their characteristics. Experienced users know how to handle each and every characteristics. This is common for race car drivers and airline pilots. If pilots do not understand an aircraft, they shouldn't be allowed to operate them.

Americans are too nice.

Important positions in the U.S. should not be filled by foreigners. Example: doctors and lawyers.

Important positions should not be fulfilled to balance gender issues. This should be done on quality and experience characteristics. No exceptions.

Immigrants that come over the border illegally should not be able to use resources intended for Americans.

The language of the U.S. is English. We should not cater to persons that do not and cannot learn it. Why Spanish? Every cereal box has information printed in Spanish. It does not have the expressive power of French and German. The English language may have some limitations, but Spanish is not the answer.

This is an important issue. Perhaps the most important of all of them. Most of us do not know what those secret organizations in the government are doing. The labeling of secret and top secret may be a way to cater to of mad scientists, who may be geniuses in their disciplines but not otherwise.

What is this Area 51 business. What do they really do? What are the results. Why should the American taxpayer pay for something with no return. Who is really/actually in this charge of it. There are other things of this nature. Going on also.

Lastly, why the subject of Artificial Intelligence is so important. Perhaps, the human race does not have the mental ability to run and take care of itself. Maybe society is on a downward slope that is getting steeper. It is possible that AI is the world's only long term solution. But people should have some say so in this regard. Perhaps, as a nation, we don't really want it. After all, we are a democratic nation. Why should the nation support all of those university and private research labs that have little or no benefit to the overall economy.

"Anyway this is what I wrote down in a hurry," said Matt. "Perhaps we can get something out of it and perhaps not. I just did not feel like taking a nap and all of it was scribbled down rather quickly."

"I like your approach, Matt," replied the General. "Sooner or later, someone has to think about things if we are to survive as a civilized society."

Ashley gave her husband a big American hug."

CHAPTER 4

ANOTHER SURPRISE

"I'm hungry," said the General.

"They say we can do what we want to do," said Ashley. "I guess we are cleared for everything. We can go to the dining room." The phone rang. Matt answered.

"Matt here," he said.

"Director Clark wants you in his office as soon as possible," said a woman. "Right now if possible."

"We will be there right away," answered Matt, and hung up. "We are on our way again. Clark wants us as soon as possible, I guess."

The threesome trudged over to the elevator and rode one floor up. Clark's office was right there so they pushed a button and the door opened. There were Bud Lewis and his wife Kathryn.

"I thought you were headed back to Russia," said the General. "What's up?"

"It's a big story," replied Bud. "I think we had better wait for Mr. Clark to sort it all out."

"Welcome, again," said Director Clark as he walked in. "We have a major problem in the intelligence directorate, and we in the final stages of winding it up. In a sense, we were all victims, but only in a sense."

"We are glad to help, if we can," said Matt. "The situation is obvious,"

"You have it figured out?" asked Clark. "Is it that obvious?"

"You have a mole in your midst, and you are in the final stages of verifying your facts," continued Matt. "When he sends a message or something, you are going to nab him."

"Not quite," said Clark. "We are going to use him."

"He knows what we are doing," said the General. "He will just relay the message and hope for then best."

"Not quite again," said Clark. "He doesn't know what we are going to with the latest project and we will reinforce him that we have no existing national plan for Artificial Intelligence, and reassign him to an out-of-way location. He will relay to Russia what we want them to believe, so in a sense, we won."

"What is Bud's position in all of this?" asked Ashley.

Clark continued. "He will go back to Russia as our military attaché, and see how things develop. He will determine what information is getting through. He is a buddy, in a sense, with the Premier."

"How do we reinforce that we are not in the process of not doing anything?" asked Matt.

"It's the other guys that were in the meeting," continued Clark. "They are having dinner in our special restaurant that we use for things like this, and then he will have a good old American vacation, and then be re-assigned to a foreign location with a rise in salary."

Matt, Ashley, and the General listened with amazement.

"This is the way we operate," said Clark. "Let me call my

wife to meet us here, and we will show the five of you how the intelligence service rewards itself. It is a fine restaurant. You can be out of here in late morning,"

The black limo pulled up to the front entrance and Mrs. Clark was already in it. Everyone climbed in, the General and Director Clark, the Lewis's, and the Miller's, and the armor plated vehicle headed to a wealthy wooded area 10 miles from the headquarters., among a group of two million dollar homes. A reliable couple and servants lived there. The home received mail as would a normal home, and the restaurant was hidden to the world. The group was escorted to a lush dining area and were seated in diplomatic style. Drinks were served. Single malt scotch to the General and Director Clark, a daiquiri to the ladies, and non-alcoholic beer to Matt and Bud. Everyone was in fine spirits. The men talked football, and the ladies talked novels and quilting.

The only thing to come out of the dinner was that the project would be wound up in the morning and they would be on the way to their respective homes by noon, except for Bud and Kathryn whose flight back to Russia was scheduled for 6 am.

CHAPTER 5

THE REAL PROJECT

The weather turned out to dull and dreary with intermittent drizzle. A perfect setting to discuss an important project with more than a few twists and turns.

"We need a name," said Clark. "It seems as though every project in this agency has a name. Unless we do not have one and it gets the informal name 'no name' that eventually becomes the full name."

"There is a fish restaurant in the Boston pier area that has the official name No Name Restaurant," said Ashley. "I wonder if it still exists."

"I have one; I mean a name," said Matt. "We will be looking for things and the is one place we Americans don't know anything about: Area 51. We could call this project Area 52."

"Boy, your brain is working like a speed demon today, Matt", said Clark.

"He's always this way," said Ashley. "He sees, remembers, and figures out everything."

"I should cover the personnel on this project," said Clark. "It is quite different than I mentioned previously. Any questions on payments, permissions, and expenses will be covered as they arise by the General and me. I have office support but he doesn't, so be nice to him."

"There will be two types of members to the team: regular members and adjuncts. Regulars get the $1 million per month plus expenses. Adjuncts get a lesser amount on a needs basis. Everyone in this room is a regular plus Buzz Bunday in England. We are all cleared. All of you are on the payroll, so to speak, as I speak. General, your wife Mme. Marguerite Purgoine is cleared. She can be on the team as a regular member if you want her. Oh, I forgot Bud and Kathryn. They are regulars."

"I do," replied the General. "I mean 'I do' to Dr. Purgoine ."

"Now, here are the adjuncts, all cleared: your former associate Harp Thomas and his wife Kimberly, that beretta carrying patrolman Harry Steevens, Kimberly Scott in Washington in addition to her regular job, Adam Benfield turned Iranian spy, and your former student-associate Robert Peterson, who we turned just last week. We are working on Wuan Singh, the Chinese math professor. Also we have the NBA player who is the friend of North Korea has been cleared. His name is Robert Friend. He is retired from basketball and probably used up all of his money. He is a nice guy and could use a little."

"Should we have been writing all of these names down?" asked Ashley.

"Don't worry about it, " said Matt softly. "I can remember them."

"One more thing," said Clark. "We have the support of Hillary Sloan, the Secretary of State. I would like for us to work with her. She a smart person and willing to assist us. She has been the First Lady for 8 years. I should have said two things. I've talked to Buzz. He will make arrangements with Katherine Penelope Radford, Prince Michael, and associates in England and Germany. Any other considerations can be worked out on the fly."

"Last but not least, the General is running the show with my assistance," said Clark. "I have a full time job around here and will provide assistance and counseling whenever I can."

"General, you are next."

"I'll be in touch with the regulars when we get a grasp on this problem," said the General. "Matt has a long list of considerations that we will distribute to you. Remember, the adjuncts are employed on a needs basis. So it is probably better not to contact them until we need their assistance, and not before. Then the only regulars that are not local are Bud, Kathryn, and Buzz. We will learn how to work together."

On the flight home in the Electric C-70, the General was pensive. Matt noticed that. At first, he thought that the General was worried that they might be recorded. The General was just extremely quiet, like he had something to say. Finally, when they were airborne and in route. He opened up.

"I have something a little embarrassing, to me anyway, to tell you. I know more about this project than you could ever imagine. Mark Carter, the President, the Secretary of State, and the Chairman of the Joint Chiefs were in on this. I have a long document that describes it. It is too long and too complicated to cover in a meeting. Also, they were measuring your reactions to it. The project is GO and I have 3 copies of the project plan in the thin leather carrier I have with me. I did not bring it with me. Clark slipped in my room. We can go through it together at your home, since the housekeeper is not cleared. Also, the project has a name that is *Deep Learning*. It refers to our learning about the enemy and the operational environment. The persons at the helm did not write it, they collectively told it to a professional writer. Unfortunately, the name is a part of the line item in the President's secret line items in the federal budget. Actually, I liked your name *Area 52* a little better and we can use it as an operational name, if you would prefer.. The line item is secret anyway, so who cares."

"They were not specific what they wanted," said Matt. "It was on purpose. I think they want us – i.e., you, Ashley, and me – to apply some interpretation to what they want. I take it as a enormous complement to our abilities. I don't really know what it is, but I am looking forward to it. I think I'll see what's in our in-flight electric kitchen."

"I bet he will come back with some pop and popcorn. He loves that old fashion language."

The flight was smooth and fast. They had to circle three times because of a beginning pilot, but it was just programmed behavior to the Electric C-70.

The threesome went directly to Matt and Ashley's home.

CHAPTER 6

GETTING STATED WITH DEEP LEARNING

Matt, Ashley and the General settled in Matt's and Ashley's house and decided to start off in the living room. Matt and Ashley took chairs and The General had the sofa. It was pleasant to be able to relax; the Langley meeting was filled with a lot of unnecessary tension.

"I love comfort," said the General as he slipped off his shoes and put his feet up..

Matt and Ashley looked at each with a smile, as if to say, 'Now this is the real General.'

"I have something to tell you," continued the General. "I don't want you to be mad at me, because this is not my doing and I was asked to keep it secret."

Matt's jaw dropped and Ashley looked at him with a half smile. Neither could think of anything to say. This definitely was not their up-front associate. He was normally the last person in the world to keep something of interest from his remarkable associates Matt and Ashley..

"I have a plan of sorts, given to me by Clark when we went to our rooms at Langley," said the General. "He just knocked at my door and handed to to me, and said 'Keep this under your hat.' It's the military was to keep your mouth shut. Don't ask me what went on before we got there because I surely do not know"

"I think this project is more serious than we originally thought," said Matt.

"That is definitely the case," replied the General. "And I do not know precisely who started it."

"We have a brand new President," responded Matt. "He has the President Daily Brief (PDF), the complicated budget, legislation, as well as all the secret stuff that's is going on. There are also a lot of secret projects going that we do not even know about."

"Like UFOs and all of that Roswell stuff that we never found out what was happening," added Ashley.

"Do you mention that citation where a UFO crashed and the Army picked up the pieces and took them to a place in Nevada that we now refer to a Area 51."

"There are all kinds of things going, such as the military equipment and new procedures that pop up up every day or two," continued Matt. "Some scientist gets some nutty idea and the Congress makes a 10 million dollar budget for it, and we never hear about it again. There are a lot of daily things that go on that we never hear about; they aren't necessarily secret but we don't have the time to find out about them until they pop up in the news."

"That's the plan," replied the General. "Apparently the President got nervous because he did not know what was going on and he couldn't trust anyone because he thought it would give him a weak reputation and the people in the Congress have vested interests. So he went to Hillary Sloan, the Secretary of State, because he felt that she would give him an unbiased view, and also she was the First Lady for 8 years. Also, her husband, the former President, would undoubtedly know a lot about the overall way the country is run and something about all of those black items that are financed but nobody know about. She is a a sharp person and recommended that maybe Artificial Intelligence might have a way of getting at the information that he thought he needed."

"That makes sense," said Matt. "If we use AI, as it is called, then we do not need a big team to dig out the information we want, just ask the computer. It doesn't doesn't have to be pin point accurate. In some cases, all we need to know is that there is something going on in a particular area."

"And we know pretty much about AI," said Ashley. "We can even ask AI for what we don't know about AI."

"I think we we are also ready to start in, that that explained why the project is so vague," said the General, "They do not know what they don't know and neither do we."

"We can start by asking AI about the key ideas and projects that are going on, and we can review the entire project and find out how to attack it," said Ashley. "We can even continue with our day jobs, as they say, and still be successful with our other employment."

"Okay," said the General. Let's just list the AI facilities, and then hit the topics the President is probably interested in. I have the feeling there will be so much information for the President that he won't be able to read all of it. Then he can review the information as his needs arise."

"I have a suspicion that we will find out why AI is so popular," said Matt. "I propose that Ashley and I take case of the AI and then get back with the General to determine exactly what we are looking for.

"Sound good Matt," answered the General. "Thanks Matt, and also Ashley."

CHAPTER 7

A SURVEY OF ARTIFICIAL INTELLIGENCE

Matt was up early the next morning. He arose expecting a call from the General; it never arrived. I guess this is not going to be a golfing day, he surmised. Probably just as tired as he and Ashley. Matt did his morning ablutions and made a couple of cups of strong coffee for himself and Ashley. She was sleeping like a log. Matt just stood there for a minute or so and finally said, "Would you like a cup of coffee?"

This was just enough to awaken Ashley who looked up with a pleasant smile.

"Sure," replied Ashley. "Especially when your are serving it."

"I'm concerned how we formulate the information that we provide to the President," said Matt. "Let's say we get the information on a subject of interest and we put it into the computer. We can categorize it in any form amenable to us. Then if he is looking for anything in particular, he has to find it. That doesn't seem so good."

"We could categorize it as we find it, and then summarize it in an appendix - perhaps in small print so it doesn't seem so long," replied Ashley. "Then we could have an index to facilitate finding items of interest."

"Actually, that is a good idea," remarked Matt. "We could

change our method on the fly. These government reports come in various forms and sizes. So let's start at Starbucks, as we usually do when we get started with a project."

So after a few minutes of prep time, off Ashley and Matt went to their favorite Starbucks. Their favorite table was free so they settled in as they did when students several years ago. The only difference was that Matt brought a notebook along just in case something interesting popped up. Nothing of particular interest did pop up.

"We have to include some introductory information on artificial intelligence," said Ashley. "Our new President may know about computers, but I doubt he knows much about AI. He was probably extra busy getting ready for the election."

"I will make a simple list of basic AI topics when we get home, and then we can start in," added Matt. "Is that seem OK without you."

"Do you think we can use one of those generative AI programs to assist us, so we don't have to look all that stuff," said Ashley. "I don't know much about AI since it isn't exactly my specialty."

"Sounds good to me," said Matt. "The only one that I know anything about is that ChatGTP that I don't know much about."

"What does Chat GTP stand for?" asked Ashley.

"I could be wrong," said Matt. "But I think that GTP is Generative Pre-Trained Transformer, and probably Chat stands for chat."

"I never used it," said Ashley. "Maybe you did."

"I did," said Matt. "I entered I think 'Hybrid car' and ChatGTP came up with a definition. Actually, it was pretty good. I should have said real good."

"Sound good to me," replied Ashley. "Let's get out of here."

CHAPTER 8

ARTIFICIAL INTELLIGENCE AWARENESS

"I think the Manner that we start of is to make a list of the key subjects in artificial intelligence and then take a quick look at what ChatGPT has to say about them," said Matt.

"Sounds good to me," replied Ashley. "Do you have a list?"

"I do," said Matt. "Here is my list and please tell me what you think about them:"

Can a machine think

Intellect behavior

Artificial general intelligence (AGI)

Singularity

Scope of AI

Intelligent systems

Cognitive technology

Virtual systems

Thinking

Learning

The Advisor model

ELIZA

Generative AI

ChatGPT

Machine learning

Cognitive computing

Ontology and AI
AI ethics
Deep learning in AI
Neural networks

"Well, what do you think about them?" said Matt.

"They look good for our purpose, but I see you have ChatGPT in the list," answered Ashley. "It could be interesting what ChatGPT has to say about itself."

"ChatGPT responses are in italics," said Matt.

Can a machine think

Machines are capable of processing information and performing tasks based on algorithms and instructions. While they can simulate human-like thinking processes through artificial intelligence, it is still debated whether machines can truly "think" in the same way humans do, with consciousness, emotions, and subjective experiences.

Intelligent Behavior

Intelligent behavior in machines refers to their ability to solve problems, learn from data, adapt to new situations, and make decisions autonomously. This is achieved through various techniques such as machine learning, natural language processing, computer vision, and more. As technology advances, machines are becoming increasingly capable of demonstrating intelligent behavior in various domains.

Artificial General Intelligence (AGI)

Artificial General Intelligence (AGI) refers to a future AI system that can understand, learn, and apply knowledge across a wide range of tasks and domains, similar to human intelligence. AGI aims to possess the same level of general cognitive abilities as humans, including reasoning, problem-solving, creativity, and emotional intelligence. While current AI technologies are specialized in narrow tasks, achieving AGI remains a long-term goal that researchers are working towards.

Singularity

The technological singularity is a hypothetical future point in time when artificial intelligence surpasses human intelligence, leading to rapid technological growth and potentially unpredictable changes in society. Some envision this event as a moment of unprecedented advancements in science, technology, and human civilization, while others warn of potential risks and ethical concerns associated with superintelligent AI. The concept of singularity has been popularized in science fiction and is a topic of ongoing debate among experts in the field of artificial intelligence.

Scope of AI

The scope of artificial intelligence is vast and continues to expand as technology advances. AI is used in various fields and applications, including but not limited to:

1. *Machine Learning: Algorithms that enable computers to learn from data and make predictions or decisions without being explicitly programmed.*

2. *Natural Language Processing: AI technologies that enable machines to understand, interpret, and generate human language.*

3. *Computer Vision: AI systems that can analyze, interpret, and understand visual information from the real world.*

4. *Robotics: The integration of AI and robotics to create autonomous machines that can perform tasks in the physical world.*

5. *Expert Systems: AI systems designed to mimic human expertise in specific domains to provide recommendations or make decisions.*

6. *AI in Healthcare: Applications of AI in medical image analysis, patient diagnosis, drug discovery, personalized medicine, and more.*

7. *AI in Finance: Applications of AI in fraud detection, algorithmic trading, risk assessment, customer service, and more.*

8. *AI in Marketing: Use of AI for personalized advertising, customer segmentation, recommendation systems, and sentiment analysis.*

9. *AI in Gaming: Use of AI for creating intelligent virtual opponents, adaptive gameplay, procedural content generation, and more.*

10. *Ethical and Social Implications of AI: Exploration of the ethical, legal, and societal impacts of AI technologies, such as bias in algorithms, privacy concerns, job displacement, and autonomous weapons.*

The scope of AI is constantly evolving as researchers and engineers push the boundaries of what is possible with artificial intelligence.

Intelligent Systems

Intelligent systems refer to AI technologies that can perceive their environment, learn from data or experience, reason about the information, and make decisions or take actions to achieve specific goals. These systems are designed to mimic human intelligence and behavior to some extent, enabling them to perform tasks that traditionally require human intelligence. Intelligent systems can range from simple rule-based systems to complex deep learning models, and they are used in various applications across industries such as healthcare, finance, marketing, transportation, and more. Some examples of intelligent systems include virtual assistants, autonomous vehicles, recommendation engines, and predictive analytics platforms. The development of intelligent systems is a growing field of research and innovation, with the goal of creating technologies that can efficiently solve complex problems and improve the quality of human life.

Cognitive Technology

Virtual systems refer to computer-based technologies that simulate physical or virtual environments for various purposes, such as training, simulation, entertainment, communication, and more. Virtual systems can include virtual reality (VR), augmented reality (AR), mixed reality (MR), and other immersive technologies that create interactive, three-dimensional experiences for users.

Virtual reality (VR) involves the use of headsets or devices to immerse users in a completely virtual environment, where they can interact with and explore different landscapes, objects, or scenarios. Augmented reality (AR) overlays digital information or objects onto the real world, enhancing the user's perception of their surroundings. Mixed reality (MR) combines elements of both virtual and real environments, allowing users to interact with digital objects in a physical space.

Virtual systems have applications in various industries, including gaming, education, healthcare, architecture, engineering, military training, and more.

They offer new ways to visualize data, train employees, simulate real-world scenarios, provide immersive experiences, and enhance communication and collaboration. As virtual systems technology continues to advance, they are expected to play an increasingly significant role in how we interact with digital content and the world around us.

Virtual Systems

Virtual systems refer to computer-based technologies that simulate physical or virtual environments for various purposes, such as training, simulation, entertainment, communication, and more. Virtual systems can include virtual reality (VR), augmented reality (AR), mixed reality (MR), and other immersive technologies that create interactive, three-dimensional experiences for users.

Virtual reality (VR) involves the use of headsets or devices to immerse users in a completely virtual environment, where they can interact with and explore different landscapes, objects, or scenarios. Augmented reality (AR) overlays digital information or objects onto the real world, enhancing the user's perception of their surroundings. Mixed reality (MR) combines elements of both virtual and real environments, allowing users to interact with digital objects in a physical space.

Virtual systems have applications in various industries, including gaming, education, healthcare, architecture, engineering, military training, and more. They offer new ways to visualize data, train employees, simulate real-world scenarios, provide immersive experiences, and enhance communication and collaboration. As virtual systems technology continues to advance, they are expected to play an increasingly significant role in how we interact with digital content and the world around us.

Thinking

"Thinking" is a complex cognitive process that involves mental activities such as reasoning, problem-solving, decision-making, imagining, and more. Human thinking is influenced by various factors, including previous experiences, beliefs, emotions, knowledge, biases, and external stimuli. The process of thinking can be conscious or unconscious, deliberate or automatic, logical or creative, and involves the manipulation of mental representations to generate ideas, make connections, and draw conclusions.

In the context of artificial intelligence, thinking refers to the ability of AI systems to simulate human thought processes and perform tasks that require intelligence, such as learning from data, making predictions, recognizing patterns, and adapting to new information. AI systems use algorithms and models to process information, infer relationships, and make decisions based on predefined rules or data patterns.

Thinking in AI involves various approaches, such as symbolic reasoning, neural networks, deep learning, probabilistic reasoning, and more, depending on the task and domain. As AI technologies continue to advance, researchers are exploring new ways to enhance AI systems' ability to think, reason, and learn in complex and dynamic environments, pushing the boundaries of what machines can achieve in terms of intelligent behavior.

Learning

Learning is a fundamental process through which individuals and systems acquire new knowledge, skills, behaviors, or attitudes. In the context of artificial intelligence, learning refers to the ability of AI systems to improve their performance on tasks through the acquisition of data, experience, or feedback. AI learning algorithms enable machines to adapt, recognize patterns, make predictions, and ultimately improve their decision-making based on the information they receive.

There are several types of learning approaches in AI, including supervised learning, unsupervised learning, reinforcement learning, and semi-supervised learning. In supervised learning, AI systems are trained on labeled data, where the correct outputs are provided to guide the learning process. Unsupervised learning involves learning patterns from unlabeled data without explicit guidance. Reinforcement learning uses feedback from the environment to learn optimal behavior through trial and error. Semi-supervised learning combines elements of both supervised and unsupervised learning approaches.

Learning in AI can involve various techniques, such as neural networks, deep learning, decision trees, support vector machines, and more, depending on the task and data at hand. AI systems learn from large datasets to recognize patterns, extract features, and make informed decisions in diverse applications, including image recognition, natural language processing, autonomous driving, healthcare, finance, and more.

The ability of AI systems to learn and adapt over time is a key factor in their success and proliferation across industries, driving innovation, automation, and efficiency in solving complex problems and improving human lives. Ongoing research and advancements in AI learning algorithms aim to further enhance the capabilities of intelligent systems and enable them to learn and perform tasks with increasing autonomy and accuracy.

The Advisor Model

The Advisor Model is a concept that refers to a framework or approach where an AI system acts as a trusted advisor or assistant to users, providing guidance, recommendations, and insights to support decision-making and problem-solving.

The Advisor Model leverages artificial intelligence technologies to analyze data, understand user preferences, and offer personalized suggestions and advice based on the context of the situation.

In the Advisor Model, AI systems use various techniques such as machine learning, natural language processing, knowledge representation, and reasoning to assist users in different domains, such as finance, healthcare, education, customer service, and more. The AI advisor analyzes data, learns from user interactions, and adapts its recommendations to meet the individual needs and goals of the user.

The goal of the Advisor Model is to enhance human capabilities by providing intelligent support and augmenting decision-making processes with data-driven insights. AI advisors can help users make more informed choices, improve efficiency, enhance productivity, and ultimately achieve better outcomes in their tasks and endeavors. By leveraging the power of AI technologies in the Advisor Model, users can access expert-level advice and assistance tailored to their specific preferences and requirements, leading to more personalized and effective interactions with intelligent systems.

ELIZA

ELIZA is a well-known early natural language processing computer program created at the MIT Artificial Intelligence Laboratory by Joseph Weizenbaum in the mid-1960s. ELIZA was designed to simulate a conversation between a human user and a computer, particularly in the context of a Rogerian psychotherapist.

ELIZA used simple pattern matching and substitution rules based on keywords to respond to user input in a way that mimicked a therapist's conversational style. The program employed techniques such as rephrasing questions as statements, reflecting user responses, and prompting further elaboration to create the illusion of understanding and empathy.

While ELIZA was limited in its ability to truly understand language or exhibit genuine intelligence, it was remarkable for its ability to engage users in conversations that seemed meaningful and human-like. ELIZA's influence on the field of artificial intelligence and human-computer interaction has been significant, inspiring further research in natural language processing, chatbots, and virtual assistants.

Despite its simplicity by today's standards, ELIZA remains a classic example of early AI experiments and a testament to the enduring fascination with creating machines that can communicate and interact with humans in a way that feels authentic and responsive.

Generative AI

Generative AI refers to a class of artificial intelligence algorithms and techniques that focus on generating new data, content, or outputs that are similar to, but not copied from, existing examples. Generative AI models are capable of creating original content, such as images, text, audio, and videos, through learning patterns and structures from a given dataset.

One popular type of generative AI model is the Generative Adversarial Network (GAN), which consists of two neural networks - a generator and a discriminator - that are trained in a competitive manner. The generator network creates new data samples, while the discriminator network evaluates these samples to distinguish between real and generated data. Through this adversarial training process, GANs can produce realistic and diverse outputs that closely resemble the training data.

Generative AI has applications in various fields, including image generation, text-to-image synthesis, music composition, video generation, and more. Creative industries, such as art, design, and entertainment, benefit from generative AI by automating content creation processes, enabling new forms of artistic expression, and facilitating the generation of novel and innovative content.

Researchers continue to explore and advance generative AI techniques to improve the realism, diversity, and controllability of generated outputs. As generative AI capabilities progress, the potential for applications in areas such as virtual reality, content creation, storytelling, and personalized user experiences expands, offering exciting possibilities for the future of artificial intelligence and creative expression.

ChatGTP

ChatGPT is a branch of AI language models developed by OpenAI that uses generative technology to generate human-like text conversation. ChatGPT leverages the power of the GPT (Generative Pre-trained Transformer) architecture, which is a type of deep learning model trained on vast amounts of text data to understand and generate human language.

ChatGPT models are designed to engage in open-ended conversations with users, responding to text inputs in a conversational manner. These AI models can understand context, generate relevant responses, and maintain coherence throughout a dialogue, making them effective in chatbot applications, language understanding tasks, and virtual assistant interactions.

The advancements in ChatGPT models have enabled more natural and contextually appropriate responses in conversational AI systems, enhancing user experiences and interactions with intelligent virtual agents. ChatGPT *models are continually being improved and fine-tuned to deliver more accurate, relevant, and engaging conversations across various domains and languages.*

Machine Learning

Machine learning is a branch of artificial intelligence that focuses on developing algorithms and models that enable computers to learn from and make predictions or decisions based on data. Instead of being explicitly programmed to perform a task, machine learning systems are trained on data to recognize patterns, extract insights, and make predictions or decisions without human intervention.

There are several types of machine learning algorithms, including supervised learning, unsupervised learning, semi-supervised learning, reinforcement learning, and deep learning. Supervised learning involves training a model on labeled data, where each data point is associated with a target variable or outcome. Unsupervised learning involves learning patterns and structures from unlabeled data, while reinforcement learning focuses on learning by interacting with an environment through trial and error.

Machine learning algorithms are used in a wide range of applications, including image and speech recognition, natural language processing, recommendation systems, healthcare diagnostics, financial forecasting, autonomous vehicles, and more. The ability of machine learning models to analyze large volumes of data, detect trends, and make informed decisions has revolutionized industries and domains, leading to improved efficiency, accuracy, and innovation.

As the field of machine learning continues to evolve, researchers and practitioners strive to develop more advanced algorithms, techniques, and models to tackle complex tasks, handle diverse types of data, and address real-world challenges. With the increasing availability of data, computing power, and expertise, machine learning is poised to drive further advancements in artificial intelligence and shape the future of technology and society.

Cognitive Computing

Cognitive computing is a branch of artificial intelligence that aims to simulate human thought processes in computer systems. Unlike traditional computing, which follows predefined instructions and rules, cognitive computing systems use machine learning, natural language processing, and other AI techniques to understand, learn, and reason like humans.

Cognitive computing systems are designed to analyze large volumes of data, extract insights, understand context, make decisions, and interact with users in a more natural and intuitive way. These systems can handle unstructured data, such as text, images, and multimedia, and adapt to new information and changing environments, making them well-suited for complex and dynamic tasks.

One prominent example of cognitive computing is IBM's Watson, a cognitive computing system that gained fame for its ability to compete on the quiz show Jeopardy! against human champions. Watson demonstrated capabilities in natural language understanding, knowledge retrieval, reasoning, and decision-making, showcasing the power of cognitive computing in processing and analyzing vast amounts of information.

Cognitive computing has applications in various fields, including healthcare, finance, customer service, education, and more. In healthcare, cognitive computing systems can assist in diagnosing diseases, recommending treatments, and analyzing medical research. In finance, these systems can analyze market trends, manage risk, and provide personalized recommendations to clients.

As cognitive computing technology advances, the potential for intelligent systems that can augment human intelligence, enhance decision-making, and facilitate interactions between humans and machines continues to grow. By combining the strengths of AI technologies with human-like cognitive abilities, cognitive computing paves the way for innovative solutions that can transform industries, drive innovation, and improve the quality of life.

Ontology and AI

Ontology, in the context of artificial intelligence, refers to the representation of knowledge about a specific domain in a structured and formalized manner. It defines the concepts, entities, relationships, and rules within a domain to facilitate knowledge sharing, reasoning, and decision-making in AI systems.

Ontologies provide a common vocabulary and taxonomy that enable AI systems to understand, interpret, and reason about the information they process. By organizing knowledge in a structured format, ontologies help AI systems handle ambiguity, infer implicit relationships, and make intelligent decisions based on the available information.

In AI applications, ontologies play a crucial role in various tasks, such as natural language processing, information retrieval, knowledge graphs, and semantic modeling. They assist in capturing domain-specific knowledge, mapping relationships between entities, resolving semantic inconsistencies, and enhancing the accuracy and efficiency of AI algorithms.

By incorporating ontologies into AI systems, developers can build more robust, flexible, and interpretable models that can effectively utilize and reason over complex information. Ontologies contribute to the development of intelligent systems that can mimic human-like cognitive processes, understand context, and draw meaningful insights from data across different domains.

Overall, the integration of ontology and AI enables more advanced and sophisticated applications that harness the power of structured knowledge representation to drive innovation, automation, and intelligence in various fields, ultimately advancing the capabilities and potential of artificial intelligence technologies.

AI Ethics

AI ethics refers to the principles, guidelines, and standards that govern the development, deployment, and use of artificial intelligence technologies in an ethical and responsible manner. As AI systems become more pervasive and powerful, ethical considerations become increasingly important to ensure that these technologies align with societal values, respect human rights, and mitigate potential risks and biases.

Key issues in AI ethics include:

1. *Bias and Fairness: AI systems can inherit biases from the data they are trained on, leading to discriminatory outcomes. Ensuring fairness and equity in AI decision-making is essential to prevent harm and uphold principles of justice.*

2. *Transparency and Explainability: Understanding how AI systems arrive at decisions is crucial for accountability, trust, and regulatory compliance. Transparency and explainability mechanisms are necessary for stakeholders to comprehend and challenge AI outcomes.*

3. *Privacy and Data Protection: AI systems often handle sensitive and personal data, raising concerns about privacy violations and data breaches. Safeguarding user data, ensuring consent, and implementing strong data protection measures are critical in AI applications.*

4. *Accountability and Responsibility: Determining who is responsible for AI decision-making and its consequences is a complex issue. Establishing clear lines of accountability, liability frameworks, and governance structures is essential to address ethical challenges in AI.*

5. *Safety and Security: Ensuring the safety and security of AI systems is paramount to prevent malicious attacks, disruptions, or unintended consequences. Robust cybersecurity measures, risk assessments, and safety protocols are vital to mitigate risks in AI deployments.*

6. *Societal Impact: Understanding the broader societal implications of AI technologies, including job displacement, economic inequality, and social polarization, is necessary to address the ethical considerations and promote inclusive and sustainable development.*

To address these ethical challenges, stakeholders, including researchers, policymakers, industry leaders, and ethicists, collaborate to develop frameworks, guidelines, and regulations that promote ethical AI practices. Initiatives such as the development of AI ethics principles, the establishment of ethical review boards, and the integration of ethics education into AI research and development efforts are crucial to foster responsible AI innovation and deployment. By upholding ethical standards and values in AI development and deployment, we can harness the potential of AI technologies to benefit society and advance human well-being.

Deep Learning in AI

Deep learning is a subset of machine learning that focuses on modeling high-level abstractions in data by using neural networks with many layers, referred to as deep neural networks. Deep learning algorithms attempt to learn multiple levels of representation of the data, with each layer in the neural network transforming the data into a more abstract and complex form.

Deep learning has gained significant attention and popularity in the field of artificial intelligence due to its ability to automatically learn features from data, handle large and complex datasets, and outperform traditional machine learning techniques in various tasks such as image and speech recognition, natural language processing, and reinforcement learning.

Key characteristics of deep learning in AI include:

1. *Neural Networks: Deep learning algorithms are typically implemented using artificial neural networks composed of multiple layers of interconnected nodes (neurons). Each layer processes the input data and learns to extract features representing different levels of abstraction.*

2. *Representation Learning: Deep learning focuses on learning representations of data through successive layers of transformations. As the data passes through the layers, the neural network automatically learns to extract relevant features from the input data.*

3. *Training with Backpropagation: Deep neural networks are trained using backpropagation, a process that involves computing the gradient of the error and updating the network's parameters to minimize the error between the predicted output and the actual output.*

4. *Deep Convolutional Networks: Convolutional neural networks (CNNs) are a type of deep neural network commonly used in image recognition tasks. CNNs leverage the spatial structure of images through convolutional layers, pooling layers, and fully connected layers to extract features and make predictions.*

5. *Recurrent Neural Networks: Recurrent neural networks (RNNs) are another type of deep learning architecture that can handle sequential data, such as text and time series. RNNs have connections that form loops, allowing them to maintain memory of previous inputs and capture temporal dependencies.*

Deep learning has revolutionized AI applications by enabling machines to learn complex patterns and representations directly from data, without the need for manual feature engineering. Advances in deep learning, coupled with the availability of large datasets and powerful hardware, have driven progress in various domains, leading to breakthroughs in image and speech recognition, natural language understanding, autonomous systems, and more.

As deep learning continues to evolve, researchers are exploring new architectures, optimization techniques, and applications to further enhance the capabilities of AI systems and unlock their potential for solving complex problems and driving innovation in diverse fields.

Neural Networks

Neural networks are a fundamental component of artificial intelligence and machine learning that are inspired by the structure and function of the human brain. They are computational models composed of interconnected nodes, called neurons, organized in layers. Neural networks are designed to learn patterns and relationships in data by adjusting their weights and biases through a process known as training.

Key concepts and components of neural networks include:

1. *Neurons: Neurons are the basic computational units in a neural network. Each neuron receives inputs, applies a transformation using weights and*

biases, and produces an output using an activation function. Neurons in one layer are connected to neurons in the next layer, forming a network.

2. Layers: Neural networks are typically organized into layers, consisting of an input layer, one or more hidden layers, and an output layer. The input layer receives data, the hidden layers process the data through transformations, and the output layer produces the final predictions or classifications.

3. Weights and Biases: The weights and biases in a neural network are parameters that are learned during the training process. They control the strength of connections between neurons and determine how input signals are transformed as they pass through the network.

4. Activation Functions: Activation functions introduce non-linearities into the neural network, allowing it to model complex relationships in data. Common activation functions include sigmoid, tanh, ReLU (Rectified Linear Unit), and softmax functions.

5. Feedforward and Backpropagation: In a feedforward neural network, data flows through the network from the input layer to the output layer. Backpropagation is an algorithm used to train neural networks by adjusting the weights and biases based on the calculated error between the predicted output and the actual output.

6. Deep Neural Networks: Deep neural networks refer to neural networks with multiple hidden layers, enabling them to learn complex patterns and hierarchies of features in data. Deep learning architectures, such as convolutional neural networks (CNNs) and recurrent neural networks (RNNs), leverage deep neural networks for tasks like image recognition and sequence modeling.

Neural networks have demonstrated remarkable capabilities in various machine learning tasks, including image and speech recognition, natural language processing, recommendation systems, and more. Their ability to learn representations of data and generalize to new examples makes them powerful tools for solving complex problems and developing intelligent systems.

As research in neural networks continues to advance, novel architectures, optimization techniques, and training algorithms are being developed to improve network performance, scalability, and interpretability. Neural networks remain a cornerstone of modern AI technologies, driving innovation and enabling the development of sophisticated solutions across a wide range of applications.

End of Chat GTP's response to Artificial Awareness words and phrases.

"Well, what do you think about the responses of ChatGTP to a few words and phrases?" asked Matt. "The italicized word just before the explanation is the query to ChatGTP."

"It looks like that is the way to go," answered Ashley. "The learning component in ChatGTP must go through millions of documents to create its responses. My personal opinion is that we are on our way to a successful project. Moreover, this generative AI concept is something that every person should know about."

CHAPTER 9

THE BASIC METHODOLOGY

"Well Ashley, we are just about ready to start on the project for the President, and before we get started, I think we should make a plan of a sorts and then bring the General into the play," said Matt. "This is a new way of doing things. Let ChatCTP do the factual work and the author does the creative part. It's like a hybrid automobile in which the engine does some things and the motor does other things. It is a matter of doing things with the most appropriate tools available. Maybe a new genre for writers."

"You're correct on that," replied Ashley. "We're authors with the objective of providing whatever is necessary, and writers do it the old way of elucidating whatever is appropriate to their field of writing. We will do the research, so to speak, and then the General will help us in choosing that which is necessary."

"This is nice," continued Matt. "We can all do what we are good at. It's like one of those capstone projects that are now appropriate in some disciplines."

"How do we start?" asked Ashley.

"I don't know exactly, but what about those TV programs where they have episodes and each one has a point of view," continued Matt.

"Like those programs on the life of the queen or a king or whoever," added Ashley. "If you miss an episode, it's still good."

"There is that thing, I don't know what they call it, where somebody investigates the secret files in the government that even the President doesn't know about. They are call black files. I saw one called Black Files: Declassified. The could be what the President is concerned about."

"I bet that's it," said Ashley.

"We could use the titles and not even look at the contents. Take the titles, as a subject, and let ChatGTP look it up for us. We aren't copying, because the titles are only subjects. The contents would come from ChatGTP and it has millions of sources and no one really knows where all the stuff comes from. The Artificial Intelligence software just puts it together, and probably on a demand basis. ChatGTP just works it out. The generative AI is pretty neat."

"Do you know how to do it?" asked Ashley.

"I have that ChatGTP on my laptop. It's free. I paid $69.99 for a new version named ChatGTP4, and it's good for a year. I used it when we got that AI stuff."

"That's pretty cheap," replied Ashley. "I bet half the world has it by now - especially the free version."

"OK, let me look up one of those TV shows," said Matt. "Anyway I'm getting hungry. Do they have sandwiches at Starbucks?"

"Let's go," said Ashley.

CHAPTER 10

SPACE FORCE

The sandwich at Starbucks was good, but Matt was too busy fiddling with his iPhone to pay any attention to it. Finally, Ashley said,"I'm going to the loo."

"Why do you continue calling the bathroom the loo?" asked Matt.

"Because it is not a room for taking a bath," said Ashley. "It's my version of analytic philosophy."

When Ashley returned, Matt casually said, "I've got our first list of ChatCPT topics. That's my version of analytic philosophy."

"That was fast," replied Ashley. "You must have cheated."

"Right," replied Matt. "Let's get back, I want to try it out."

Back at the ranch, so to speak, Matt went directly to his laptop, and in less than 5 minutes he sent a list of my items to his printer. He smiled when he gave a copy to Ashley. Here is what it looked like: (The chapter title comes from the first entry)

Secrets of the Space Force
American UFOs
To Catch an Alien
Iron Man
Army Night stalkers

"What do you think," asked Matt. "It seems to be a good start. The ChatGPY queries look appropriate to our project. The President should be concerned with the various topics."

"Look good to me, but I don't know much about those things," replied Ashley.

"I would guess that is the power of artificial intelligence," answered Matt.

Secrets of the Space Force

As an AI assistant, I don't have access to classified information or secrets related to the Space Force or any other governmental or military organization. The United States Space Force is a branch of the U.S. Armed Forces responsible for space operations and ensuring the security and defense of U.S. interests in space. While there may be ongoing projects, initiatives, or developments within the Space Force that are not publicly disclosed for security reasons, it is important to respect the confidentiality and national security of such information.

If you have any questions about the Space Force or space-related topics that are publicly available, I would be happy to provide information and insights to the best of my knowledge. Feel free to ask about any non-classified aspects of the Space Force or space exploration, and I'll do my best to assist you!

+What is the Objective of the Space Force

The United States Space Force, established as the sixth branch of the U.S. Armed Forces in December 2019, has several primary objectives focused on ensuring U.S. superiority in space operations and protecting national interests in the space domain. Some key objectives of the Space Force include:

1. *Space Superiority: The Space Force aims to maintain U.S. dominance in space by developing, acquiring, and operating space capabilities that support national security objectives. This includes protecting U.S. space assets, such as satellites, from threats and ensuring freedom of action in space.*

2. *Space Operations: The Space Force is responsible for organizing, training, and equipping space forces to conduct a wide range of space-related operations, including satellite communications, missile warning systems, surveillance, and navigation services.*

3. *National Security: Protecting U.S. national security interests in space is a critical mission of the Space Force. This involves monitoring and responding to potential threats in space, such as anti-satellite weapons, cyber attacks, and other hostile actions that could impact U.S. space capabilities.*

4. *Space Awareness: The Space Force is tasked with improving situational awareness in space by tracking and monitoring objects in orbit, providing early warning of potential hazards, and ensuring the safety and security of space operations.*

5. *International Partnerships: The Space Force collaborates with international allies and partners to promote peaceful and responsible behavior in space, strengthen space cooperation, and enhance space domain awareness through information sharing and joint activities.*

6. *Innovation and Technology Development: To maintain its technological edge in space, the Space Force invests in research, development, and innovation to advance space capabilities, enhance resilience, and address emerging challenges in the space domain.*

Overall, the primary objective of the U.S. Space Force is to protect U.S. interests in space, ensure the security and sustainability of space operations, and maintain leadership in space capabilities to support national security and defense priorities. By focusing on space superiority, operations, security, awareness, international partnerships, and innovation, the Space Force plays a critical role in safeguarding U.S. interests in the increasingly contested and congested space environment.

+How Large in Personnel in the Space Force

As of 2021, the United States Space Force, the newest branch of the U.S. Armed Forces, is still in the process of building its personnel size and organizational structure. The Space Force was officially established in December 2019 with the goal of consolidating and coordinating space-related operations within the military.

The exact number of personnel in the Space Force may vary over time as the branch continues to grow and expand its workforce. While specific figures may not be readily available due to the dynamic nature of military personnel assignments and deployments, the Space Force is comprised of a combination of active-duty military personnel, civilian professionals, and possibly members transitioning from other branches of the military.

The Space Force's focus on space-related operations, technological expertise, and specialized training for space missions requires a workforce with diverse skill sets in areas such as space operations, satellite communications, missile warning systems, cybersecurity, intelligence, engineering, and more.

As the Space Force continues to evolve and establish its presence in the U.S. military landscape, it is expected to grow in size and capabilities with the recruitment and training of personnel dedicated to space operations, national security in space, and advancing U.S. interests in the space domain. The Space Force's personnel numbers and structure will likely continue to develop in the coming years to support its mission objectives and operational requirements in this critical and evolving domain.

American UFOs

Unidentified Flying Objects (UFOs) have been a topic of interest and speculation for decades, with reported sightings and encounters sparking curiosity and debate about the possibility of extraterrestrial life and advanced aerial phenomena. The U.S. government and military have investigated UFO reports over the years, and in recent times, there has been increased public awareness and discussion around unidentified aerial phenomena (UAPs) or "American UFOs."

In 2020, the U.S. Department of Defense established the Unidentified Aerial Phenomena Task Force to investigate and assess UAP sightings reported by military personnel and the general public. The task force aims to gather and analyze data on UAP sightings to determine if these phenomena pose any potential threats to national security or if they can be explained by known sources.

In June 2021, the Office of the Director of National Intelligence released a report to Congress on UAPs, providing a summary of UAP sightings and acknowledging that some of these aerial phenomena remain unexplained. The report highlighted the need for further investigation and research to better understand the nature and origin of UAPs.

It's important to note that while some UFO sightings have been attributed to natural phenomena, weather events, human-made objects, or misidentifications, there are cases that continue to defy conventional explanations. The study *of UFOs and UAPs involves a complex and multidisciplinary approach, encompassing scientific analysis, data collection, witness testimonies, and collaboration between governmental agencies, research organizations, and academia.*

As interest in UFOs and UAPs persists, ongoing efforts to study and analyze these phenomena with a scientific and evidence-based approach are crucial to advancing our understanding of the unexplained aerial sightings and potentially uncovering new insights about the mysteries of the universe. Whether these sightings have earthly or extraterrestrial origins, the investigation of UFOs and UAPs remains a fascinating and important area of research that captures the imagination of people around the world.

To Catch an Alien

"To Catch an Alien" sounds like an intriguing concept that could be explored in various forms of entertainment, such as books, films, TV shows, or games. The idea of capturing or encountering an alien being raises questions about interspecies communication, ethical considerations, scientific exploration, and potentially even interstellar diplomacy.

In a fictional context, a story titled "To Catch an Alien" could follow a group of scientists, explorers, or government agents who discover evidence of extraterrestrial life and embark on a mission to interact with or capture an alien entity for study. This narrative could delve into themes of curiosity, the unknown, the search for truth, and the challenges of bridging the gap between humans and beings from another world.

The storyline could involve elements of mystery, suspense, and discovery as the characters navigate encounters with alien technology, behaviors, and environments. Ethical dilemmas may arise regarding the treatment of alien life forms, the consequences of interplanetary contact, and the implications for humanity's place in the universe.

During the journey to catch an alien, the characters could face obstacles, conflicts, and moral choices that shape their understanding of the alien being and their own beliefs about life beyond Earth. The narrative could offer a thought-provoking exploration of what it means to encounter the unknown and how such encounters could impact individuals, societies, and the future of humanity's relationship with the cosmos.

Overall, "To Catch an Alien" has the potential to be a compelling and captivating story that invites audiences to ponder the possibilities of alien life, the mysteries of the universe, and the profound implications of contact with beings from distant worlds. Whether in a work of fiction or as a thought experiment, the idea of catching an alien sparks imagination, wonder, and a sense of adventure in exploring the boundaries of what lies beyond our planet.

How to Stop an Assassination

Preventing or stopping an assassination is a complex and serious matter that requires careful planning, coordination, and risk management. If you believe there is a threat of an assassination attempt, here are some general steps that could be taken to enhance security and reduce the risk:

1. ***Security Assessment***: *Conduct a thorough security assessment to identify potential vulnerabilities and threats. Evaluate the individual or location that may be targeted for an assassination attempt.*

2. ***Increased Security Measures***: *Enhance physical security measures, such as increasing the number of security personnel, implementing access controls, installing surveillance systems, and conducting regular security patrols.*

3. **Risk Mitigation Strategies**: Develop risk mitigation strategies based on the specific threat assessment. This could include implementing protective measures, changing routines, and establishing emergency response plans.

4. **Intelligence Gathering**: Collect intelligence on potential threats and individuals or groups that may be planning the assassination. Stay vigilant and monitor for any suspicious activities or behavior.

5. **Security Briefings**: Provide security briefings to individuals at risk of being targeted for assassination. Educate them on personal safety measures, threat awareness, and emergency response protocols.

6. **Collaboration with Law Enforcement**: Work closely with law enforcement agencies to share threat information, coordinate security efforts, and seek assistance in preventing any potential attacks.

7. **Communication Protocols**: Establish communication protocols for reporting suspicious activities, threats, or security incidents. Encourage individuals to report any concerning behavior promptly.

8. **Training and Drills**: Conduct security training sessions and emergency drills to prepare individuals for responding to potential threats, attacks, or emergencies effectively.

9. **Public Awareness**: If the threat of an assassination is high-profile, consider increasing public awareness and communication about the potential risks and security measures in place to protect individuals.

10. **Seek Professional Assistance**: In cases of credible threats or imminent danger, consider seeking assistance from professional security consultants,

threat assessment experts, or law enforcement agencies with expertise in protective services.

It's important to note that every situation is unique, and the specific measures taken to stop an assassination will depend on the nature of the threat, the individuals involved, and the resources available. Prioritizing security, threat assessment, communication, and proactive prevention strategies are key to mitigating risks and ensuring the safety of individuals at risk of being targeted for an assassination.

Iron Man Army

The concept of an Iron Man army could involve the development and deployment of a fleet of advanced robotic suits or exoskeletons inspired by the iconic Iron Man suit from the Marvel Universe. These suits could be designed to enhance the capabilities of military forces, law enforcement agencies, or emergency responders in various operational scenarios.

Here are some potential features and applications of an Iron Man army:

1. **Enhanced Strength and Mobility**: *The suits could provide wearers with superhuman strength, agility, and speed, enabling them to perform physically demanding tasks and maneuvers with ease.*

2. **Integrated Weapons Systems**: *Equipped with advanced weaponry such as repulsors, missiles, energy blasters, and other high-tech armaments, the suits could be formidable combat units on the battlefield.*

3. **Advanced Sensors and Targeting Systems**: *Built-in sensors, targeting systems, and heads-up displays could enhance situational awareness, accuracy, and decision-making for users during missions.*

4. **Durability and Protection**: *The suits could be armored with advanced materials capable of withstanding ballistic, energy-based, and environmental threats to protect users from harm.*

5. **Flight Capabilities**: *Some iterations of the Iron Man army suits could feature flight systems, allowing wearers to navigate and engage targets from the air.*

6. **Medical and Emergency Response Features**: *Incorporating medical sensors, communication systems, and life-saving capabilities could make the suits valuable assets for search and rescue missions, disaster response efforts, and medical evacuations.*

7. **Customization and Adaptability**: *Modular design elements and customization options could allow users to tailor the suits to their specific needs and preferences for different mission profiles.*

While the concept of an Iron Man army offers exciting possibilities for enhancing operational capabilities and protecting personnel in challenging environments, it also raises ethical, legal, and strategic considerations. Questions about control, oversight, autonomy, accountability, and the impact of advanced technology on warfare would need to be carefully addressed when designing and deploying such systems.

Ultimately, the development of an Iron Man army would require extensive research, development, testing, and evaluation to ensure the effectiveness, safety, and ethical use of these advanced technologies in support of national security, public safety, and humanitarian efforts.

Nightstalkers

The Nightstalkers are a fictional organization that has appeared in various forms of media, including movies, television shows, comic books, and video games. In different contexts, the Nightstalkers may refer to different groups or individuals with specific roles and characteristics. One notable depiction of the Nightstalkers is in the Marvel Comics universe, where they are a team of supernatural specialists who hunt vampires and other mystical threats.

In the 1998 film "Blade: Trinity," the Nightstalkers are a group of vampire hunters led by Hannibal King, Abigail Whistler, and the legendary vampire hunter Blade. The Nightstalkers use advanced weapons, technology, and combat skills to battle vampires and other supernatural creatures in an ongoing struggle to protect humanity from the forces of darkness.

In military terminology, Night Stalkers may refer to the 160th Special Operations Aviation Regiment (Airborne), a U.S. Army special operations unit known for conducting nighttime missions, often involving helicopter-based operations in support of special operations forces.

Overall, whether in fiction or reality, the name Nightstalkers carries connotations of darkness, stealth, specialization, and a willingness to confront threats in the shadows. The concept of night operations, clandestine missions, and facing formidable adversaries under cover of darkness adds intrigue and mystery to the persona of the Nightstalkers across different storytelling mediums.

"This seems to be quite useful," said Ashley. "Some of the information is superfluous but I would say that represents life in general."

"The plus sign just before a query denotes that it is a subset, of the original query," said Matt. "Logically, one should class all of the information together."

CHAPTER 11

ROBOTS

"This section deals with robots, and I think the idea is that is a way of preserving human personnel, and also robots can sometimes do things a human cannot do," said Matt.

"It looks like a popular subject from the number of subjects:"

Future Robotic Warfare
Secrets of the Paranormal
Secrets World of Mind Control
Presidential Power Secrets
Mystery of Mission 7
Secrets Paranormal Research
Secrets of Drone Warfare

Future Robotic Warfare

The future of robotic warfare presents a complex landscape shaped by advances in technology, ethical considerations, international regulations, and strategic implications. As robotic systems continue to evolve and become more sophisticated, they are likely to play an increasingly significant role in modern warfare. Here are some key aspects to consider regarding future robotic warfare:

1.   **Autonomous Systems**: *Autonomous robots and drones equipped with artificial intelligence could be deployed for a range of military applications, including reconnaissance, surveillance, target acquisition,*

and even decision-making in combat situations. The development of fully autonomous weapons raises ethical questions about accountability, human control, and the potential for unintended consequences.

2. **Swarm Robotics**: Swarm robotics involves coordinating multiple robots to work together towards a common goal. In a military context, swarm robots could be used for tasks such as surveillance, search and rescue missions, or even coordinated attacks on enemy targets. The ability to deploy swarms of robots could provide a tactical advantage on the battlefield.

3. **Unmanned Aerial Vehicles (UAVs)**: Drones have already become a prominent feature of modern warfare, offering capabilities for intelligence, surveillance, reconnaissance, and precision strikes. Future UAVs may feature advanced stealth, endurance, speed, and autonomous operation, transforming the nature of aerial warfare.

4. **Ground Robotics**: Ground robots could be used for tasks such as logistics support, demining operations, patrolling, and combat roles on the battlefield. These robots could enhance

Secrets of the Paranormal

The paranormal is a realm of mysterious phenomena and unexplained experiences that fascinate and intrigue many individuals. While the secrets of the paranormal remain elusive and often defy scientific explanation, there are several key themes and concepts often associated with this field:

1. **Ghosts**: One of the most well-known aspects of the paranormal, ghosts are believed to be spirits or entities of the dead that linger in the physical world. Reports of ghostly apparitions, unexplained noises, and

strange occurrences in supposedly haunted locations have fueled interest in ghost hunting and paranormal investigation.

2. **UFOs and Extraterrestrial Life**: Unidentified Flying Objects (UFOs) and claims of encounters with extraterrestrial beings have long captured the public imagination. The search for evidence of alien visitations, government cover-ups, and the existence of intelligent life beyond Earth continues to be a topic of debate and speculation.

3. **Psychic Abilities**: Psychic phenomena, such as telepathy, clairvoyance, precognition, and psychokinesis, suggest the existence of capabilities that transcend conventional scientific understanding. Individuals claiming psychic abilities have been studied and researched to explore the potential of extrasensory perception.

4. **Cryptids and Monsters**: Cryptids are creatures of folklore and legend that are said to exist but have not been scientifically proven. Examples include Bigfoot, the Loch Ness Monster, and the Chupacabra. Sightings and encounters with these mysterious beings fuel interest in cryptozoology and the search for undiscovered species.

5. **Parapsychology**: Parapsychology is the study of paranormal phenomena using scientific methods. Researchers in this field investigate topics such as telepathy, psychokinesis, near-death experiences, and hauntings, seeking to understand the nature of these phenomena and their potential implications for our understanding of consciousness and reality.

6. **Ancient Mysteries**: The paranormal is often intertwined with ancient mysteries, such as lost civilizations, archaeological enigmas, and unexplained phenomena from the distant past. The exploration of ancient sites, artifacts, and texts can offer insights into the unexplained and the supernatural.

While the paranormal remains a realm of speculation, belief, and mystery, it continues to spark curiosity and inspire exploration into the unknown. The search for answers and the quest to unravel the secrets of the paranormal reflect humanity's enduring fascination with the unexplained and the supernatural.

Secret World of Mind control

The concept of mind control, also known as brainwashing or thought manipulation, has long been a subject of intrigue and speculation in popular culture, psychology, and conspiracy theories. The idea of influencing or controlling someone's thoughts, beliefs, and behaviors without their consent raises ethical, psychological, and philosophical questions about the nature of free will and autonomy. Here are some key aspects of the secret world of mind control:

1. **Historical Context**: *Mind control techniques have been explored and employed throughout history, often in the context of warfare, espionage, cults, and propaganda. Methods such as psychological manipulation, hypnosis, drugs, and coercive persuasion have been used to influence individuals and groups for various purposes.*

2. **Psychological Manipulation**: *Psychological techniques, such as gaslighting, persuasion, and emotional manipulation, can be used to exert control over someone's thoughts and behaviors. Cults, abusive relationships, and authoritarian regimes are known to employ tactics that undermine an individual's sense of reality and agency.*

3. **Subliminal Messaging**: *The use of subliminal messages, hidden cues, and suggestive imagery in media and advertising has raised concerns about the potential for subconscious influence on people's preferences,*

attitudes, and behaviors. The effectiveness and ethics of subliminal messaging remain topics of debate among psychologists and media experts.

4. ***Cognitive Control**: Advances in neuroscience and cognitive science have led to research on techniques for modulating cognitive functions and influencing decision-making processes. Brain stimulation, neurofeedback, and cognitive enhancement technologies raise questions about the boundaries of ethical behavior and the potential for unintended consequences.*

5. ***Conspiracy Theories**: The idea of secret government programs, covert organizations, and clandestine experiments involving mind control has given rise to numerous conspiracy theories. Stories of alleged mind control experiments, such as the CIA's MKUltra program, spark debate and speculation about the extent of human manipulation.*

6. ***Ethical Considerations**: The ethical implications of mind control raise profound questions about privacy, consent, autonomy, and the limits of psychological influence. Safeguarding individual rights, promoting informed consent, and upholding ethical standards in research and practice are essential in addressing concerns related to mind control.*

While the secret world of mind control remains shrouded in mystery and controversy, exploring the ethical, psychological, and societal dimensions of influence and persuasion can deepen our understanding of human behavior and the complexities of cognitive manipulation. Understanding the mechanisms of mind control and its implications can help individuals recognize and resist undue influence while promoting transparency, critical thinking, and ethical decision-making.

HARRY KATZAN JR.

Presidential Power Secrets

The exercise of presidential power is a complex and multifaceted aspect of government that involves a combination of constitutional authority, political influence, institutional norms, and public perception. While some aspects of presidential power are enshrined in the Constitution, there are also certain nuances, practices, and strategies that can be considered "secrets" of presidential power. Here are some key insights into the exercise of presidential power:

1. **Executive Orders**: *One of the lesser-known "secrets" of presidential power is the use of executive orders, which allow the president to dictate policy without congressional approval. Executive orders can be a powerful tool for shaping domestic and foreign policy, bypassing legislative gridlock, and responding quickly to emergent issues.*

2. **National Security Directives**: *National Security Presidential Memoranda (NSPMs) and National Security Council Directives (NSCDs) are classified documents that outline the president's decisions and directives on national security matters. These documents play a crucial role in shaping the administration's security and foreign policy strategies.*

3. **Political Appointments**: *The president's power to appoint individuals to key positions within the executive branch, including cabinet members, judges, and agency heads, can have a significant impact on policy implementation and decision-making. Leveraging these appointments strategically can influence the direction of government operations.*

4. **Informal Powers**: *Informal powers, such as the president's ability to set the policy agenda, shape public opinion, and engage in diplomatic initiatives, can have a profound impact on the exercise of presidential*

power. These informal tools of influence often complement formal constitutional powers.

5.   **Presidential Communication**: *Effective communication strategies, including public speeches, press conferences, social media, and other forms of outreach, are essential for conveying the president's priorities, goals, and initiatives to the public and shaping public perception.*

6.   **Presidential Pardons**: *The president's power to grant pardons and commutations can be a secretive and powerful tool for exercising executive clemency, influencing legal outcomes, and shaping perceptions of justice and mercy.*

While the exercise of presidential power is subject to checks and balances from other branches of government, the president's ability to wield formal and informal tools of influence can shape policy outcomes, public opinion, and the direction of the nation. Understanding the complexities and nuances of presidential power can provide insights into the dynamics of governance and the exercise of authority in a democratic society.

USS Jimmy Carter

The USS Jimmy Carter (SSN-23) is a U.S. Navy Seawolf-class nuclear-powered submarine. It is named after the 39th President of the United States, Jimmy Carter. Commissioned in 2005, the USS Jimmy Carter is known for its unique modifications and capabilities, which have led to speculation about its special missions and operations.

One of the most notable features of the USS Jimmy Carter is its extended hull section, known as the Multi-Mission Platform (MMP). This section provides additional space for a variety of missions, including intelligence gathering, underwater operations, and special forces deployments. The submarine's enhanced flexibility and versatility make it well-suited for classified missions and strategic activities.

Given its advanced technology and secretive nature, the USS Jimmy Carter has attracted curiosity and speculation about its potential roles and missions, leading to its reputation as a highly specialized and secretive asset within the U.S. Navy's submarine fleet.

Secret Paranormal Research

The world of secret paranormal research is a realm shrouded in mystery and intrigue, often involving investigations into phenomena beyond the scope of conventional science. This clandestine field may encompass a variety of activities, including the study of ghosts, UFOs, cryptids, psychic abilities, and other mysterious occurrences.

In this obscure world of supernatural inquiry, researchers might delve into haunted locations, conduct experiments to test psychic phenomena, analyze unexplained sightings, and explore ancient legends and myths. The secrecy surrounding these investigations could be attributed to the potential consequences of revealing information that challenges mainstream beliefs or poses unexplained phenomena.

Secret paranormal research may involve collaboration with government agencies, private organizations, or independent researchers with specialized knowledge in the supernatural. The goal of such research could be to unlock the secrets of the unexplained, uncover hidden truths about the nature of reality, or even harness paranormal phenomena for various purposes.

While the existence of covert paranormal research projects remains largely speculative, the allure of the unknown and the possibility of unlocking the mysteries of the supernatural continue to captivate the imagination of those who venture into this enigmatic realm of exploration and discovery.

Secrets of Drone Warfare

Drone warfare, also known as unmanned aerial vehicle (UAV) warfare, has revolutionized modern military operations, offering both advantages and ethical challenges. Here are some of the key aspects and secrets surrounding drone warfare:

1. **Precision and Targeted Strikes**: *One of the main advantages of drone warfare is the ability to conduct precise and targeted strikes against enemy targets, minimizing collateral damage compared to traditional methods of warfare.*

2. **Surveillance and Reconnaissance**: *Drones are used extensively for surveillance and reconnaissance missions, providing real-time intelligence to military forces. This enables commanders to make informed decisions and better plan military operations.*

3. **Secret Missions and Covert Operations**: *Drones are often used in secret missions and covert operations to gather intelligence, track high-value targets, and conduct airstrikes without direct engagement of ground forces.*

4. **Remote Piloting**: *Drone operators can control the aircraft from a remote location, often thousands of miles away from the actual battlefield. This enables 24/7 surveillance and strike capabilities, but also raises ethical concerns about the detachment of warfare from the human experience.*

5. **Legal and Ethical Challenges**: *Drone warfare has sparked debates about its legality, ethical implications, and risks of civilian casualties. The secrecy surrounding drone operations can sometimes lead to accountability issues and questions about transparency.*

6. **Advancements in Technology**: *The development of artificial intelligence, machine learning, and autonomous drones is shaping the future of drone warfare, potentially raising concerns about the implications of autonomous weapons systems.*

While drone warfare offers strategic advantages in modern military operations, the secrecy surrounding its use, the ethical dilemmas it raises, and the potential for unintended consequences highlight the need for careful consideration and scrutiny of this evolving form of warfare.

"This section did not seem to be as useful as the earlier ones," said Ashley. "Does that mean that we just do not have access to it?"

"I think that is the case," replied Matt. "I guess that we, the ChatGPT system, and just about everyone including the President is totally locked out of the Black Files. I'm not so sure that is good. We have another collection of episodes and maybe we will come up with something that could be use to the President. I think that he should not be locked out of any files in the U.S. arsenal."

CHAPTER 12

TERRORISM AND CRIMINALS

"This is our last section," said Matt. "I think we should give a heads up to the General that we will have something for him in the very near future. He might be curious about what we are doing, so you had better make the call to him, because he never gets mad at you. He likes to give me a cold shoulder when he is not to happy. On the other hand, I wonder what in the world could he be doing."

"He might be in Washington digging up something else for us to do," replied Ashley. "I don't think that down deep he gets all of the work that we perform for him. He's like the students who think all we have to do is to hold the class and then go out and surf for the afternoon. But, I'll call and give him my sweet treatment."

Fifteen minutes later, Ashley return with no news. He didn't even answer.

"Let's wrap this up, and then head on out. Here are the subjects; they do not look to bad:

Tracking Terror: The 9/11 Plot.

The Norte Valley Cartel

The Terrorist Next Door: Operation Smokescreen

Hunting War Criminals

The Spy Game: Russian Espionage

HARRY KATZAN JR.

Buried Secrets: Unbreakable Codes
The Merchant of Death: Viktor Bout
Operation Firewall: The Takedown of Shadow crew

Tracking Terror: The 9/11 Plot

The 9/11 terrorist attacks, which occurred on September 11, 2001, were a series of coordinated suicide attacks carried out by the extremist group al-Qaeda against the United States. Here are some key points about the 9/11 plot:

1. ***Planning and Coordination***: *The 9/11 attacks were meticulously planned and coordinated by al-Qaeda operatives, with the mastermind identified as Khalid Sheikh Mohammed. The attackers were trained in flying commercial aircraft and carried out the attacks with precision.*

2. ***Terrorist Hijackings***: *On the morning of September 11, 2001, 19 hijackers took control of four commercial airplanes. They intentionally crashed two planes into the World Trade Center towers in New York City, one into the Pentagon in Arlington, Virginia, and the fourth plane, United Airlines Flight 93, crashed in a field in Pennsylvania after passengers attempted to overcome the hijackers.*

3. ***Casualties and Impact***: *The 9/11 attacks resulted in the deaths of nearly 3,000 people and caused significant destruction and devastation. The attacks had far-reaching consequences, leading to a global war on terror, changes in U.S. national security policies, and increased vigilance in counterterrorism efforts worldwide.*

4. ***Investigations and Aftermath***: *Following the attacks, extensive investigations were conducted to identify the perpetrators, accomplices, and*

80

sources of support. The U.S. government launched military campaigns in Afghanistan and later in Iraq as part of the response to the attacks.

5. ★★*Legacy and Remembrance*★★: *The 9/11 attacks left a lasting impact on the United States and the world, shaping policies on national security, counterterrorism, surveillance, and immigration. The day is commemorated annually as a national day of remembrance and serves as a reminder of the resilience and unity in the face of tragedy.*

The 9/11 plot stands as a tragic chapter in global history, underscoring the persistent threat of terrorism and the importance of international cooperation in combating extremist ideologies and enhancing security measures to prevent future attacks.

The Norte Valle Cartel

The Norte Valley Cartel is a fictional criminal organization often depicted in movies, TV shows, books, and other forms of entertainment. While not based on a real criminal group, the Norte Valley Cartel is typically portrayed as a powerful and ruthless drug cartel operating in a fictional region, blending elements of organized crime, corruption, violence, and intrigue.

In fictional depictions, the Norte Valley Cartel is often characterized by its control of the drug trade, financial resources, influence over local authorities, and willingness to resort to extreme measures to protect its interests and maintain dominance in the criminal underworld. Stories involving the Norte Valley Cartel may explore themes such as loyalty, betrayal, power struggles, and the human cost of involvement in illicit activities.

The portrayal of the Norte Valley Cartel in fiction serves to create compelling narratives, explore complex characters, and engage audiences with thrilling and suspenseful storylines. While not a real criminal organization, the

Norte Valley Cartel exemplifies the fascination with crime dramas and the exploration of the darker aspects of human nature in storytelling.

The Terrorist Next Door: Operation Smokescreen

"Operation Smokescreen" is a hypothetical scenario involving a fictional terrorist plot orchestrated by a shadowy extremist group with connections to domestic terrorism. In this fictional narrative, the terrorist organization operates covertly within a community, blending in with everyday life while secretly planning and preparing for a major attack.

Key elements of "Operation Smokescreen" might include:

1. ***Infiltration and Radicalization**: The terrorist group infiltrates the community, recruiting and radicalizing individuals to carry out their deadly mission. Members of the group may appear as ordinary neighbors, coworkers, or acquaintances, hiding their true intentions behind a facade of normalcy.*

2. ***Covert Planning and Preparation**: The terrorists carefully plan and prepare for their attack, using encrypted communications, safe houses, and anonymous funding sources to avoid detection by authorities. They may acquire weapons, explosives, and logistics while operating under the radar.*

3. ***Surveillance and Reconnaissance**: The terrorists conduct surveillance on potential targets, gathering intelligence and assessing vulnerabilities to maximize the impact of their attack. They may monitor security measures, patterns of life, and response times of authorities to exploit weaknesses in the system.*

4. **False Flags and Misdirection**: As part of "Operation Smokescreen," the terrorists may deploy tactics of misinformation, false flags, and misdirection to confuse law enforcement agencies and divert attention away from their true intentions. By sowing confusion and chaos, they aim to create cover for their nefarious activities.

5. **Counterterrorism Response**: Law enforcement and intelligence agencies, in collaboration with community members, work tirelessly to uncover the terrorist plot, disrupt the operation, and prevent the attack. Through surveillance, intelligence analysis, and coordinated efforts, they strive to bring the terrorists to justice and prevent loss of life.

"Operation Smokescreen" serves as a fictional narrative that explores the themes of terrorism, national security, community resilience, and the complexities of combating violent extremism. By delving into the hypothetical scenario of a terrorist threat emerging from within a community, this storyline underscores the importance of vigilance, cooperation, and preparedness in safeguarding against acts of terrorism.

Hunting War Criminals

Hunting war criminals is a challenging and complex task that involves international cooperation, legal frameworks, intelligence gathering, and dedicated efforts by law enforcement agencies and international tribunals. Here are some key aspects of hunting war criminals:

1. **Identification and Investigation**: The first step in hunting war criminals is to identify individuals suspected of committing war crimes, crimes against humanity, or genocide. This often involves collecting evidence, conducting interviews, and analyzing testimonies to build cases against perpetrators.

2. **International Tribunals**: International bodies such as the International Criminal Court (ICC), the International Criminal Tribunal for the former Yugoslavia (ICTY), and the International Criminal Tribunal for Rwanda (ICTR) play a crucial role in prosecuting war criminals and holding them accountable for their actions.

3. **National Jurisdictions**: National courts and legal systems also have a responsibility to prosecute war criminals under the principle of universal jurisdiction, allowing countries to prosecute individuals for serious crimes regardless of where the crimes were committed.

4. **Cooperation and Extradition**: Hunting war criminals often requires international cooperation, extradition treaties, and diplomatic efforts to apprehend suspects and transfer them to the appropriate jurisdiction for prosecution. This can be a lengthy and complex process, especially when suspects are located in different countries.

5. **Intelligence and Surveillance**: Law enforcement agencies and intelligence services use advanced technologies, surveillance methods, and investigative techniques to track down war criminals who may be hiding in remote locations or using false identities to evade capture.

6. **Public Awareness and Advocacy**: Public awareness campaigns, advocacy efforts, and grassroots movements play a vital role in raising awareness about war crimes, promoting justice for victims, and pressuring governments to prioritize the apprehension and prosecution of war criminals.

Hunting war criminals is a critical aspect of upholding international humanitarian law, seeking justice for victims of atrocities, and deterring future crimes against humanity. By pursuing accountability for those responsible for war crimes, the international community sends a powerful message that impunity will not be tolerated, and that perpetrators will be held accountable for their actions.

The Spy Game: Russian Espionage

Russian espionage has a long and storied history, dating back to the days of the Soviet Union and continuing into the present day. Russian intelligence agencies, such as the Foreign Intelligence Service (SVR) and the Main Intelligence Directorate (GRU), are known for their sophisticated and aggressive espionage operations around the world.

Here are some key aspects of Russian espionage:

1. **Historical Context**: Russian espionage has deep roots in history, with the Soviet era marked by the activities of infamous intelligence agencies like the KGB. Cold War espionage between the Soviet Union and the United States was characterized by high-stakes operations, double agents, and deep cover spies.

2. **Modern Operations**: Russian espionage continues to be a significant concern for Western intelligence agencies. The SVR and the GRU are known for their activities in gathering intelligence, conducting cyber operations, and engaging in covert influence campaigns to further Russia's strategic interests.

3. **Cyber Espionage**: Russia is known for its advanced capabilities in cyber espionage, including hacking, disinformation campaigns, and online influence operations. Russian hackers have been linked to cyber attacks on government agencies, businesses, and critical infrastructure in various countries.

4. **Illegals Program**: The "Illegals Program," as famously portrayed in the TV series "The Americans," involved Russian spies operating under deep cover in foreign countries, assuming false identities and blending into society to gather intelligence and carry out covert operations.

5. **Espionage Tradecraft**: Russian spies are trained in a range of espionage tradecraft, including surveillance, covert communication methods, document forgery, and psychological manipulation. They are skilled in the art of espionage and deception, using a combination of technology and human intelligence to achieve their objectives.

6. **Counterintelligence Efforts**: Western intelligence agencies, such as the CIA, MI6, and European counterparts, actively monitor and counter Russian espionage activities through surveillance, intelligence analysis, and efforts to disrupt and deter Russian intelligence operations.

Russian espionage remains a significant aspect of global security threats, with ongoing concerns about Russian interference in elections, cyber attacks, and intelligence gathering activities. Understanding the tactics, capabilities, and motivations of Russian intelligence agencies is crucial for defending against and countering the threats posed by Russian espionage.

Buried Secrets: Unbreakable Codes

"Buried Secrets: Unbreakable Codes" suggests a compelling narrative involving hidden messages, cryptic communications, and the challenge of cracking seemingly unbreakable codes. This fictional storyline could explore the world of cryptography, espionage, and intrigue, weaving together themes of mystery, deception, and the quest for hidden knowledge.

In this hypothetical scenario, "Buried Secrets" could center around a cryptic message or encoded information that holds the key to a long-buried secret *or valuable treasure. The protagonist, perhaps a skilled cryptographer or codebreaker, becomes entangled in a web of deception as they race against time to decipher the unbreakable code and unravel the mystery.*

Key elements of the storyline could include:

1. ***The Cryptic Message**: The story kicks off with the discovery of a cryptic message, encrypted using a sophisticated and seemingly unbreakable code. The message hints at a hidden treasure, a dangerous conspiracy, or a long-forgotten secret that could change everything.*

2. ***The Codebreaker**: The protagonist, a brilliant codebreaker with a knack for unraveling complex ciphers, is recruited to decipher the mysterious code. Armed with their expertise in cryptography and a keen eye for patterns, the codebreaker delves into the intricate world of encryption to crack the code and reveal its secrets.*

3. ***Espionage and Intrigue**: As the codebreaker delves deeper into the encrypted message, they attract the attention of shadowy figures, rival cryptographers, and perhaps even intelligence agencies vying to control the valuable information hidden within the code. The stakes are high, and danger lurks around every corner.*

4. ***Decoding the Mystery**: Through a series of twists and turns, the codebreaker follows a trail of clues, breaks through layers of encryption, and uncovers the truth behind the cryptic message. The race against time intensifies as enemies close in, leading to a climactic showdown that could change the course of history.*

5. ***Themes of Trust and Betrayal**: Along the way, the codebreaker must navigate a web of deception, betrayal, and shifting alliances as they*

seek to unlock the secrets hidden within the unbreakable code. Who can be trusted, and who is working against them in their quest for the truth?

"Buried Secrets: Unbreakable Codes" offers a captivating premise for a thrilling tale of mystery, suspense, and intellectual challenge, blending elements of cryptography, espionage, and high-stakes intrigue. It explores the timeless fascination with hidden messages, unsolved mysteries, and the power of knowledge, inviting audiences to embark on a thrilling journey into the world of codebreaking and discovery.

CHAPTER 13

ADDITIONAL SUBJECTS

"I have 7 additional subjects that could be useful in our report to the President," said Matt."Do you want to take a look at them?"

"Of course," said Ashley. "I don't any idea whatsoever about how many subjects are enough. This is foreign territory to me."

"Here they are:"

Night Stalkers
Night Vision Technology
Military Drones
Hypersonic Unmanned Vehicles
Skunk Works
Project Star
Red Cell Team

Night Stalkers

"Night Stalkers" conjures up images of stealth, darkness, and danger, suggesting a story filled with intrigue, suspense, and high-octane action. This title could be used for a fictional work that follows a specialized group of elite operatives or a covert tactical unit who operate under the cover of darkness to carry out daring missions and confront formidable enemies.

In this hypothetical scenario, "Night Stalkers" could be a thrilling tale of bravery, sacrifice, and heroism as the team navigates treacherous situations, faces overwhelming odds, and battles against insurmountable challenges. The narrative could explore themes of loyalty, camaraderie, and the human cost of warfare as the Night Stalkers embark on missions that push them to their limits.

Key elements of the storyline could include:

1. ***Special Operations**: The Night Stalkers could be a highly trained and specialized unit within the military or a government agency, tasked with executing classified missions that require precision, stealth, and swift action under the cover of darkness.*

2. ***Dangerous Missions**: The Night Stalkers could be deployed to hotspots around the world to conduct rescue operations, gather intelligence, eliminate high-value targets, or thwart terrorist threats. Their missions could take them into hostile territory, where they must rely on their training, wits, and teamwork to survive.*

3. ***Intrigue and Betrayal**: As the Night Stalkers face formidable adversaries and navigate complex political landscapes, they may encounter betrayal, deception, and moral dilemmas that test their resolve and question the boundaries of operations.*

Night Vision Technology

Night vision technology has revolutionized the way we see and operate in low-light or nighttime environments, enabling enhanced visibility and surveillance capabilities in situations where natural light is limited. This advanced technology amplifies ambient light or infrared radiation, allowing users to see in the dark with clarity and detail that would otherwise be impossible.

In fictional storytelling, "Night Vision Technology" could serve as a compelling theme or plot device to create suspenseful and action-packed scenarios. Here are some ways this theme could be incorporated into a narrative:

1. **Military Thriller**: The story could follow a special operations team equipped with cutting-edge night vision technology on a high-stakes mission behind enemy lines. The use of night vision goggles, scopes, and thermal imaging devices could add a layer of tension and realism to the action-packed sequences as the team navigates through darkness to achieve their objective.

2. **Survival Adventure**: In a survival or wilderness adventure story, characters could rely on night vision equipment to navigate through a dark and dangerous landscape, evading threats and uncovering hidden dangers as they strive to survive. The juxtaposition of light and shadow could create a visually striking backdrop for the characters' journey.

3. **Mystery or Thriller**: Night vision technology could play a key role in unraveling a mystery or uncovering hidden secrets in a suspenseful narrative. A detective or investigator equipped with night vision gear could piece together clues in the shadows, revealing a clandestine plot or solving a crime that unfolds under the cover of darkness.

4. **Sci-Fi or Futuristic Setting**: Set in a futuristic world, a sci-fi story could explore the implications of advanced night vision technology, perhaps featuring characters with cybernetic enhancements that grant them enhanced vision capabilities in all lighting conditions. This futuristic twist could lead to unique storytelling opportunities and intriguing world-building.

91

Overall, "Night Vision Technology" presents a versatile and dynamic theme that can add depth, excitement, and intrigue to a wide range of fictional narratives, from military thrillers to sci-fi adventures and beyond. Its ability to illuminate the unseen and unveil hidden truths makes it a compelling element for crafting immersive and engaging stories.

Military Drones

Military drones, also known as unmanned aerial vehicles (UAVs), have revolutionized modern warfare with their capabilities for reconnaissance, surveillance, and targeted strikes. These advanced aerial systems can be operated remotely, providing military forces with valuable intelligence, precision firepower, and strategic advantages on the battlefield.

In fictional storytelling, "Military Drones" could serve as a compelling theme or plot device to explore the ethical, tactical, and political implications of unmanned warfare. Here are some ways this theme could be incorporated into a narrative:

1. ***Political Intrigue**: A fictional story could center around a high-stakes political conflict where military drones play a pivotal role in shaping the outcome. The narrative could delve into debates over the morality of drone warfare, the consequences of remote-controlled attacks, and the complex decision-making processes involved in using these advanced technologies.*

2. ***Technological Thriller**: In a fast-paced thriller, military drones could be hacked or repurposed by rogue actors, leading to a series of escalating crises and high-octane action sequences. The protagonist could be a skilled drone pilot racing against time to prevent a catastrophic attack orchestrated by a shadowy adversary.*

3. **Human vs. Machine**: *The narrative could explore the themes of man versus machine, as characters grapple with the psychological, moral, and emotional implications of using drones in combat. The story could delve into the human cost of remote warfare, as well as the blurred boundaries between autonomy and control in a world where machines make life-and-death decisions.*

4. **Future Warfare**: *Set in a futuristic world, a sci-fi story could imagine a landscape dominated by autonomous military drones, where humans and machines coexist in a complex web of alliances and conflicts. The narrative could explore themes of artificial intelligence, autonomy, and the evolution of warfare in an age of technological advancements.*

Overall, "Military Drones" presents a thought-provoking and timely theme that can add depth, tension, and moral complexity to fictional narratives across genres. Its portrayal of cutting-edge technology, ethical dilemmas, and the changing nature of warfare offers ample storytelling opportunities to explore the intersection of humanity and machines in a world shaped by innovation and conflict.

Hypersonic Unmanned Vehicles

Hypersonic unmanned vehicles represent a cutting-edge technology that combines the high-speed capabilities of hypersonic aircraft with the unmanned, autonomous operation of drones. These advanced vehicles can travel at speeds exceeding Mach 5, allowing for rapid response times, long-range missions, and high maneuverability in both military and civilian applications.

In fictional storytelling, "Hypersonic Unmanned Vehicles" offer a wealth of creative possibilities and narrative intrigue. Here are some ways this concept could be incorporated into a story:

1. **Military Thriller**: *The story could follow a covert military operation centered around a hypersonic unmanned vehicle equipped with advanced weaponry and surveillance capabilities. As the vehicle navigates high-speed missions in hostile territories, the protagonist must grapple with the ethical dilemmas of autonomous warfare and the implications of deploying cutting-edge technology in combat.*

2. **Espionage Adventure**: *In a high-stakes espionage narrative, rival intelligence agencies could race to acquire a top-secret hypersonic drone prototype with game-changing capabilities. The fast-paced story could unfold as agents engage in clandestine operations, high-speed chases, and daring heists to secure or sabotage the futuristic technology.*

3. **Search and Rescue Drama**: *Set in a near-future world, the story could focus on a team of emergency responders utilizing hypersonic unmanned vehicles to conduct rapid search and rescue missions in disaster-stricken areas. The narrative could explore themes of heroism, innovation, and the lifesaving potential of cutting-edge technology in times of crisis.*

4. **Space Exploration Saga**: *Venturing into the realm of science fiction, the narrative could imagine a future where hypersonic unmanned vehicles are used for interstellar travel,*

Skunk Works

The term "Skunk Works" originated from a top-secret research and development facility established by Lockheed Martin in the 1940s. This facility, located in Burbank, California, was responsible for developing cutting-edge aircraft designs, including the iconic U-2 spy plane and the SR-71 Blackbird, among others. The name "Skunk Works" was inspired by the Al Capp comic strip "Li'l Abner," where a fictional moonshine factory was called "Skonk Works."

The Skunk Works team was known for its unconventional approach to innovation, working quickly and collaboratively to tackle complex engineering challenges and deliver groundbreaking aircraft designs. The group operated with a high level of autonomy and secrecy, often pushing the boundaries of technology and engineering to create aircraft that were ahead of their time.

Over the years, the Skunk Works concept has become synonymous with high-performance, cutting-edge technology development in a fast-paced and creative environment. The term is now used more broadly to refer to any innovative and agile project team that operates outside of traditional organizational structures to achieve ambitious goals.

In fiction, "Skunk Works" can evoke themes of innovation, secrecy, expertise, and high-stakes challenges. Stories inspired by the concept of Skunk Works may explore the world of advanced technology, espionage, and unconventional problem-solving in a high-pressure environment. Whether set in the realm of aerospace engineering, military operations, or futuristic worlds, narratives featuring a Skunk Works-like organization can captivate readers with tales of daring innovation, brilliant minds at work, and the thrill of pushing the limits of what is possible.

Project Star

"Project Star" could evoke a sense of grandeur, mystery, and ambition in fictional storytelling. This name suggests a top-secret, high-stakes endeavor that involves astronomical proportions, whether in the realms of science, exploration, or innovation. Here are some ways "Project Star" could be incorporated into a compelling narrative:

1. **Space Exploration Epic**: *"Project Star" could serve as the code name for a groundbreaking mission to explore deep space, discover new planets, or unravel the mysteries of the universe. The story could follow a diverse crew of astronauts, scientists, and engineers as they embark on a perilous journey beyond the stars, encountering cosmic wonders, alien civilizations, and profound revelations along the way.*

2. **Advanced Technology Initiative**: *In a near-future world, "Project Star" could represent a cutting-edge research program focused on developing revolutionary technologies for space travel, energy generation, or communication with extraterrestrial life. The narrative could delve into the scientific breakthroughs, ethical dilemmas, and geopolitical tensions surrounding this ambitious project.*

3. **Apocalyptic Scenario**: *"Project Star" could be the last-ditch effort to save humanity from a cataclysmic event, such as a global pandemic, asteroid impact, or environmental collapse. The story could follow a group of survivors working on the project to build a starship, space colony, or other refuge to ensure the continuation of the human species in the face of impending doom.*

4. **Secret Government Experiment**: *"Project Star" could be a clandestine government initiative shrouded in conspiracy, intrigue, and danger. The narrative could center on a whistleblower, journalist, or insider seeking to expose the truth behind the project's true purpose, whether it involves advanced weaponry, mind control experiments, or contact with extraterrestrial beings.*

Overall, "Project Star" offers a versatile and evocative concept that can spark imaginative narratives across genres, from epic space operas to gritty conspiracies, exploring themes of exploration, innovation, survival, and the quest for knowledge in a vast and mysterious universe.

Red Cell Team

A "Red Cell Team" typically refers to a specialized group within an organization that is tasked with conducting simulated attacks or security assessments to test vulnerabilities, identify weaknesses, and enhance preparedness. This concept is often used in the military, intelligence agencies, cybersecurity firms, and other high-security organizations to assess their defenses and response capabilities in the face of potential threats.

In fictional storytelling, a "Red Cell Team" can be a compelling element to explore themes of intrigue, strategy, and high-stakes challenges. Here are some ways this concept could be incorporated into a story:

1. **Espionage Thriller**: The story could revolve around a covert Red Cell Team operating in the shadows to infiltrate rival intelligence agencies, corporate headquarters, or government facilities. As the team executes intricate simulations and tests, they uncover a conspiracy that threatens global security, leading to a complex web of deception, betrayal, and espionage.

2. **Heist Adventure**: In a high-octane caper narrative, a Red Cell Team could be hired to orchestrate a simulated heist on a museum, bank, or high-security facility to test the defenses and vulnerabilities of the target. The story unfolds as the team navigates intricate security measures, outwits rival criminals, and races against time to pull off the ultimate simulation.

3. **Cybersecurity Drama**: Set in the world of digital warfare and cyber espionage, the story could follow a Red Cell Team tasked with conducting

simulated cyber-attacks on critical infrastructure, government networks, or corporate systems to test their resilience against virtual threats. As the team delves into the dark web, decodes encrypted messages, and engages in virtual combat, they uncover a cyber conspiracy with far-reaching consequences.

4. **Survival Challenge**: In a post-apocalyptic setting, a Red Cell Team could be part of a survival experiment where individuals are tasked with testing their skills, resourcefulness, and teamwork in extreme conditions. The story could explore themes of resilience, ingenuity, and the human spirit as the team faces harsh environments, deadly challenges, and moral dilemmas to prove their worth in a world turned upside down.

Whether set in the world of espionage, cyber warfare, heists, or survival challenges, a "Red Cell Team" offers a dynamic narrative device to explore themes of strategy, teamwork, risk-taking, and the ever-evolving nature of security and defense in a complex and unpredictable world.

"Well that is it," said Matt with a big smile on his face."

CHAPTER 14

THE GENERAL

Matt and Ashley printed out everything they had on project **Deep Learning** and headed out to see then General, who was ostensibly at home.

The General's house keeper said she didn't know where the General was and also when he would be back.

"He is probably at the driving range," said Matt. "He will be back when he gets tired."

"Why would he go to the driving range?" asked Ashley.

"Because you played better than he at the Intelligence 9-hole course," answered Matt.   "He's got that World War II mentality about women. He'll get over it."

At just about that time, the General appeared. He looked tired.

"Oh hello," said then General. "I didn't know you would be here. You should have called."

"We have good news for you," said Ashley.

"We have solved our problem and the President's information problem has been resolved," said Matt. "At least, from our point of view."

Happy to hear that," replied the General. "I don't fancy that project at all. How did you do it so quickly?"

"We used AI," answered Ashley.

"It was that package named ChatGPT," said Matt. "We got a few relevant subjects from TV and a couple of books, and then we entered those subjects into ChatGPT and got the results we needed for the President's report. It's done."

"What does that ChatGPT stand for?" asked the General.

"GPT is Generative Pre-Trained Transformer and Chat is from an old term Chatbot," remarked Ashley.

"I read about that," said the General. "It's something you use, just like a computer. You need things like that to do different things. Like IBM computers. If Henry Ford had made cars that can only do certain things like go to the supermarket, go to school, and go to church, then we wouldn't have all of these great cars we have today."

"You're impressive, Sir," said Matt. "Where did you learn about all of this AI stuff?"

"From those 3 books you used in our other projects; they are on my nightstand," replied the General."

"What books are they?" asked Ashley

"There are three of them," said the General. "Do you want their names?"

"Sure do," answered Ashley.

"Get some paper to write down the titles:

On the Trail of Artificial Intelligence
Advanced Lessons in Artificial Intelligence
Conspectus of Artificial Intelligence

Said the General. The *Lessons* book even contains a primer to go. The is just like that cooking book titled *Lessons in*

Chemistry written by that lady who even had a TV show on the subject."

"Well, I'll be,". Said Matt. "Will you please take care of getting our report to the persons involved?"

"You bet, said the General., "May I invite the two of you to have a dinner at the Green Room. I will invite Anna."

CHAPTER 15

PRESIDENTIAL REPORT

Confidential

FINAL REPORT ON THE DEEP
LEARNING PROJECT

General Remarks

The mission originates at the highest level of the U.S. government.

The implication is that the U.S. government is doing well, relatively speaking, but it could do better because some of its problems are inherent in the system itself.

A specific example is that there is a general impression that the U.S. way is the best way. Maybe the only way.

Examples are in the area of business, and it results in the notion the U.S. is the only country that knows all there is to know about design, development, engineering, production, sales, and support. This feeling is from Americans.

Americans are the only ones that have brains and others are necessarily not intelligent.

HARRY KATZAN JR.

It is true that Americans have evolved well in the sense that smart people marry and have smart children, and so forth. This is not the necessarily the case worldwide. Just a thought.

Americans think they are the only nation that knows about international relations.

The U.S. is the only country that knows how to fight wars, even though the allies in World War II (e.g., Russia) did very well indeed.

The U.S. is totally hung up on human rights.

The U.S. is the only country that knows anything about Artificial Intelligence, medicine, vaccines, epidemics, food preparation, and alcoholic beverages.

There are two countries, e.g., England and the U.S., that think they know what is best and should run the show. Especially England, and they do not like Americans. They often regard the U.S. as the colonies.

Propaganda exists in all nations. It is part of a strategy.

Other countries blame the U.S. for every problem that exists in the wide world.

Many Americans have come from foreign countries. They are not bad. Their work ethic is more than satisfactory.

Other countries steal technology from the U.S., including medicine, agriculture, and banking. When a worldwide problem arises, they wait for the U.S. to solve it.

104

Many persons come to the U.S. for various reason, and then criticize the U.S. No one has asked them to come here.

Many persons from foreign think they know how to run the U.S. and do not know anything about the situation. The U.S. should do this and that. It is not their business.

Americans should be getting tired of this and say so.

Americans think they know everything. In many cases and subjects, they do.

People from other counties do stupid things and expect the U.S. to support and help them out. They start wars and all kinds of other stuff. I expand on this later.

Many foreigners bring their social customs with them, and refuse to change. They think the U.S. should change for them.

Many counties criticize the U.S. but don't like it when Americans criticize them.

Foreigners think that they know how Americans should think and operate, when they do not understand the issues .

The U.S. supports most of the international organizations. Foreign countries expect help but do not pay their share.

The U.S. gives a lot of foreign aid and get nothing in return, except big trouble.

American should be careful with outsourcing to some foreign countries.

Foreigners should not be allowed to purchase U.S. assets, like China in the Midwest.

Foreigners should not be allowed to fly American airplanes, when they can't read the manuals. Also, some are two stupid to fly American planes.

Airplanes have exit doors in case of accidents. Airlines eliminate those doors to gain two or three seats. Foreign outsourcers do not understand this form of American stupidity when it exists. They do not understand American so-called logic that the customer gets what they want, even though it might not be the best of ideas.

Every mechanical device from washing machines to airplanes have their characteristics. Experienced users know how to handle each and every characteristics. This is common for race car drivers and airline pilots. If pilots do not understand an aircraft, they shouldn't be allowed to operate them.

Americans are too nice.

Important positions in the U.S. should not be filled by foreigners. Example: doctors and lawyers.

Important positions should not be fulfilled to balance gender issues. This should be done on quality and experience characteristics. No exceptions.

Immigrants that come over the border illegally should not be able to use resources intended for Americans.

The language of the U.S. is English. We should not cater to persons that do not and cannot learn it. Why Spanish? Every cereal box has information printed in Spanish. It does not have the expressive power of French and

German. *The English language may have some limitations, but Spanish is not the answer.*

This is an important issue. Perhaps the most important of all of them. Most of us do not know what those secret organizations in the government are doing. The labeling of secret and top secret may be a way to cater to of mad scientists, who may be geniuses in their disciplines but not otherwise.

What is this Area 51 business. What do they really do? What are the results. Why should the American taxpayer pay for something with no return. Who is really/actually in this charge of it. There are other things of this nature. Going on also.

Lastly, why the subject of Artificial Intelligence is so important. Perhaps, the human race does not have the mental ability to run and take care of itself. Maybe society is on a downward slope that is getting steeper. It is possible that AI is the world's only long term solution. But people should have some say so in this regard. Perhaps, as a nation, we don't really want it. After all, we are a democratic nation. Why should the nation support all of those university and private research labs that have little or no benefit to the overall economy.

Artificial Intelligence

Intelligent Behavior

Intelligent behavior in machines refers to their ability to solve problems, learn from data, adapt to new situations, and make decisions autonomously. This is achieved through various techniques such as machine learning, natural language processing, computer vision, and more. As technology advances, machines are becoming increasingly capable of demonstrating intelligent behavior in various domains.

Artificial General Intelligence (AGI)

Artificial General Intelligence (AGI) refers to a future AI system that can understand, learn, and apply knowledge across a wide range of tasks and domains, similar to human intelligence. AGI aims to possess the same level of general cognitive abilities as humans, including reasoning, problem-solving, creativity, and emotional intelligence. While current AI technologies are specialized in narrow tasks, achieving AGI remains a long-term goal that researchers are working towards.

Singularity

The technological singularity is a hypothetical future point in time when artificial intelligence surpasses human intelligence, leading to rapid technological growth and potentially unpredictable changes in society. Some envision this event as a moment of unprecedented advancements in science, technology, and human civilization, while others warn of potential risks and ethical concerns associated with superintelligent AI. The concept of singularity has been popularized in science fiction and is a topic of ongoing debate among experts in the field of artificial intelligence.

Scope of AI

The scope of artificial intelligence is vast and continues to expand as technology advances. AI is used in various fields and applications, including but not limited to:

1. *Machine Learning: Algorithms that enable computers to learn from data and make predictions or decisions without being explicitly programmed.*

2. *Natural Language Processing: AI technologies that enable machines to understand, interpret, and generate human language.*

3. *Computer Vision: AI systems that can analyze, interpret, and understand visual information from the real world.*

4. *Robotics: The integration of AI and robotics to create autonomous machines that can perform tasks in the physical world.*

5. *Expert Systems: AI systems designed to mimic human expertise in specific domains to provide recommendations or make decisions.*

6. *AI in Healthcare: Applications of AI in medical image analysis, patient diagnosis, drug discovery, personalized medicine, and more.*

7. *AI in Finance: Applications of AI in fraud detection, algorithmic trading, risk assessment, customer service, and more.*

8. *AI in Marketing: Use of AI for personalized advertising, customer segmentation, recommendation systems, and sentiment analysis.*

9. *AI in Gaming: Use of AI for creating intelligent virtual opponents, adaptive gameplay, procedural content generation, and more.*

10. *Ethical and Social Implications of AI: Exploration of the ethical, legal, and societal impacts of AI technologies, such as bias in algorithms, privacy concerns, job displacement, and autonomous weapons.*

The scope of AI is constantly evolving as researchers and engineers push the boundaries of what is possible with artificial intelligence.

Intelligent Systems

Intelligent systems refer to AI technologies that can perceive their environment, learn from data or experience, reason about the information, and make decisions or take actions to achieve specific goals. These systems are designed to mimic human intelligence and behavior to some extent, enabling them to perform tasks that traditionally require human intelligence. Intelligent systems can range from simple rule-based systems to complex deep learning models, and they are used in various applications across industries such as healthcare, finance, marketing, transportation, and more. Some examples of intelligent systems include virtual assistants, autonomous vehicles, recommendation engines, and predictive analytics platforms. The development of intelligent systems is a growing field of research and innovation, with the goal of creating technologies that can efficiently solve complex problems and improve the quality of human life.

<u>Cognitive Technology</u>

Virtual systems refer to computer-based technologies that simulate physical or virtual environments for various purposes, such as training, simulation, entertainment, communication, and more. Virtual systems can include virtual reality (VR), augmented reality (AR), mixed reality (MR), and other immersive technologies that create interactive, three-dimensional experiences for users.

Virtual reality (VR) involves the use of headsets or devices to immerse users in a completely virtual environment, where they can interact with and explore different landscapes, objects, or scenarios. Augmented reality (AR) overlays digital information or objects onto the real world, enhancing the user's perception of their surroundings. Mixed reality (MR) combines elements of both virtual and real environments, allowing users to interact with digital objects in a physical space.

Virtual systems have applications in various industries, including gaming, education, healthcare, architecture, engineering, military training, and more.

They offer new ways to visualize data, train employees, simulate real-world scenarios, provide immersive experiences, and enhance communication and collaboration. As virtual systems technology continues to advance, they are expected to play an increasingly significant role in how we interact with digital content and the world around us.

Virtual Systems

Virtual systems refer to computer-based technologies that simulate physical or virtual environments for various purposes, such as training, simulation, entertainment, communication, and more. Virtual systems can include virtual reality (VR), augmented reality (AR), mixed reality (MR), and other immersive technologies that create interactive, three-dimensional experiences for users.

Virtual reality (VR) involves the use of headsets or devices to immerse users in a completely virtual environment, where they can interact with and explore different landscapes, objects, or scenarios. Augmented reality (AR) overlays digital information or objects onto the real world, enhancing the user's perception of their surroundings. Mixed reality (MR) combines elements of both virtual and real environments, allowing users to interact with digital objects in a physical space.

Virtual systems have applications in various industries, including gaming, education, healthcare, architecture, engineering, military training, and more. They offer new ways to visualize data, train employees, simulate real-world scenarios, provide immersive experiences, and enhance communication and collaboration. As virtual systems technology continues to advance, they are expected to play an increasingly significant role in how we interact with digital content and the world around us.

Thinking

"Thinking" is a complex cognitive process that involves mental activities such as reasoning, problem-solving, decision-making, imagining, and more. Human thinking is influenced by various factors, including previous experiences, beliefs, emotions, knowledge, biases, and external stimuli. The process of thinking can be conscious or unconscious, deliberate or automatic, logical or creative, and involves the manipulation of mental representations to generate ideas, make connections, and draw conclusions.

In the context of artificial intelligence, thinking refers to the ability of AI systems to simulate human thought processes and perform tasks that require intelligence, such as learning from data, making predictions, recognizing patterns, and adapting to new information. AI systems use algorithms and models to process information, infer relationships, and make decisions based on predefined rules or data patterns.

Thinking in AI involves various approaches, such as symbolic reasoning, neural networks, deep learning, probabilistic reasoning, and more, depending on the task and domain. As AI technologies continue to advance, researchers are exploring new ways to enhance AI systems' ability to think, reason, and learn in complex and dynamic environments, pushing the boundaries of what machines can achieve in terms of intelligent behavior.

Learning

Learning is a fundamental process through which individuals and systems acquire new knowledge, skills, behaviors, or attitudes. In the context of artificial intelligence, learning refers to the ability of AI systems to improve their performance on tasks through the acquisition of data, experience, or feedback. AI learning algorithms enable machines to adapt, recognize patterns, make predictions, and ultimately improve their decision-making based on the information they receive.

There are several types of learning approaches in AI, including supervised learning, unsupervised learning, reinforcement learning, and semi-supervised learning. In supervised learning, AI systems are trained on labeled data, where the correct outputs are provided to guide the learning process. Unsupervised learning involves learning patterns from unlabeled data without explicit guidance. Reinforcement learning uses feedback from the environment to learn optimal behavior through trial and error. Semi-supervised learning combines elements of both supervised and unsupervised learning approaches.

Learning in AI can involve various techniques, such as neural networks, deep learning, decision trees, support vector machines, and more, depending on the task and data at hand. AI systems learn from large datasets to recognize patterns, extract features, and make informed decisions in diverse applications, including image recognition, natural language processing, autonomous driving, healthcare, finance, and more.

The ability of AI systems to learn and adapt over time is a key factor in their success and proliferation across industries, driving innovation, automation, and efficiency in solving complex problems and improving human lives. Ongoing research and advancements in AI learning algorithms aim to further enhance the capabilities of intelligent systems and enable them to learn and perform tasks with increasing autonomy and accuracy.

The Advisor Model

The Advisor Model is a concept that refers to a framework or approach where an AI system acts as a trusted advisor or assistant to users, providing guidance, recommendations, and insights to support decision-making and problem-solving.

The Advisor Model leverages artificial intelligence technologies to analyze data, understand user preferences, and offer personalized suggestions and advice based on the context of the situation.

In the Advisor Model, AI systems use various techniques such as machine learning, natural language processing, knowledge representation, and reasoning to assist users in different domains, such as finance, healthcare, education, customer service, and more. The AI advisor analyzes data, learns from user interactions, and adapts its recommendations to meet the individual needs and goals of the user.

The goal of the Advisor Model is to enhance human capabilities by providing intelligent support and augmenting decision-making processes with data-driven insights. AI advisors can help users make more informed choices, improve efficiency, enhance productivity, and ultimately achieve better outcomes in their tasks and endeavors. By leveraging the power of AI technologies in the Advisor Model, users can access expert-level advice and assistance tailored to their specific preferences and requirements, leading to more personalized and effective interactions with intelligent systems.

ELIZA

ELIZA is a well-known early natural language processing computer program created at the MIT Artificial Intelligence Laboratory by Joseph Weizenbaum in the mid-1960s. ELIZA was designed to simulate a conversation between a human user and a computer, particularly in the context of a Rogerian psychotherapist.

ELIZA used simple pattern matching and substitution rules based on keywords to respond to user input in a way that mimicked a therapist's conversational style. The program employed techniques such as rephrasing questions as statements, reflecting user responses, and prompting further elaboration to create the illusion of understanding and empathy.

While ELIZA was limited in its ability to truly understand language or exhibit genuine intelligence, it was remarkable for its ability to engage users in conversations that seemed meaningful and human-like. ELIZA's influence on the field of artificial intelligence and human-computer interaction has been significant, inspiring further research in natural language processing, chatbots, and virtual assistants.

Despite its simplicity by today's standards, ELIZA remains a classic example of early AI experiments and a testament to the enduring fascination with creating machines that can communicate and interact with humans in a way that feels authentic and responsive.

Generative AI

Generative AI refers to a class of artificial intelligence algorithms and techniques that focus on generating new data, content, or outputs that are similar to, but not copied from, existing examples. Generative AI models are capable of creating original content, such as images, text, audio, and videos, through learning patterns and structures from a given dataset.

One popular type of generative AI model is the Generative Adversarial Network (GAN), which consists of two neural networks - a generator and a discriminator - that are trained in a competitive manner. The generator network creates new data samples, while the discriminator network evaluates these samples to distinguish between real and generated data. Through this adversarial training process, GANs can produce realistic and diverse outputs that closely resemble the training data.

Generative AI has applications in various fields, including image generation, text-to-image synthesis, music composition, video generation, and more. Creative industries, such as art, design, and entertainment, benefit from generative AI by automating content creation processes, enabling new forms of artistic expression, and facilitating the generation of novel and innovative content.

Researchers continue to explore and advance generative AI techniques to improve the realism, diversity, and controllability of generated outputs. As generative AI capabilities progress, the potential for applications in areas such as virtual reality, content creation, storytelling, and personalized user experiences expands, offering exciting possibilities for the future of artificial intelligence and creative expression.

ChatGTP

ChatGPT is a branch of AI language models developed by OpenAI that uses generative technology to generate human-like text conversation. ChatGPT leverages the power of the GPT (Generative Pre-trained Transformer) architecture, which is a type of deep learning model trained on vast amounts of text data to understand and generate human language.

ChatGPT models are designed to engage in open-ended conversations with users, responding to text inputs in a conversational manner. These AI models can understand context, generate relevant responses, and maintain coherence throughout a dialogue, making them effective in chatbot applications, language understanding tasks, and virtual assistant interactions.

The advancements in ChatGPT models have enabled more natural and contextually appropriate responses in conversational AI systems, enhancing user experiences and interactions with intelligent virtual agents. ChatGPT models are continually being improved and fine-tuned to deliver more accurate, relevant, and engaging conversations across various domains and languages.

Machine Learning

Machine learning is a branch of artificial intelligence that focuses on developing algorithms and models that enable computers to learn from and make predictions or decisions based on data. Instead of being explicitly programmed to perform a task, machine learning systems are trained on data to recognize patterns, extract insights, and make predictions or decisions without human intervention.

There are several types of machine learning algorithms, including supervised learning, unsupervised learning, semi-supervised learning, reinforcement learning, and deep learning. Supervised learning involves training a model on labeled data, where each data point is associated with a target variable or outcome. Unsupervised learning involves learning patterns and structures from unlabeled data, while reinforcement learning focuses on learning by interacting with an environment through trial and error.

Machine learning algorithms are used in a wide range of applications, including image and speech recognition, natural language processing, recommendation systems, healthcare diagnostics, financial forecasting, autonomous vehicles, and more. The ability of machine learning models to analyze large volumes of data, detect trends, and make informed decisions has revolutionized industries and domains, leading to improved efficiency, accuracy, and innovation.

As the field of machine learning continues to evolve, researchers and practitioners strive to develop more advanced algorithms, techniques, and models to tackle complex tasks, handle diverse types of data, and address real-world challenges. With the increasing availability of data, computing power, and expertise, machine learning is poised to drive further advancements in artificial intelligence and shape the future of technology and society.

Cognitive Computing

Cognitive computing is a branch of artificial intelligence that aims to simulate human thought processes in computer systems. Unlike traditional computing, which follows predefined instructions and rules, cognitive computing systems use machine learning, natural language processing, and other AI techniques to understand, learn, and reason like humans.

Cognitive computing systems are designed to analyze large volumes of data, extract insights, understand context, make decisions, and interact with users in a more natural and intuitive way. These systems can handle unstructured data, such as text, images, and multimedia, and adapt to new information and changing environments, making them well-suited for complex and dynamic tasks.

One prominent example of cognitive computing is IBM's Watson, a cognitive computing system that gained fame for its ability to compete on the quiz show Jeopardy! against human champions. Watson demonstrated capabilities in natural language understanding, knowledge retrieval, reasoning, and decision-making, showcasing the power of cognitive computing in processing and analyzing vast amounts of information.

Cognitive computing has applications in various fields, including healthcare, finance, customer service, education, and more. In healthcare, cognitive computing systems can assist in diagnosing diseases, recommending treatments, and analyzing medical research. In finance, these systems can analyze market trends, manage risk, and provide personalized recommendations to clients.

As cognitive computing technology advances, the potential for intelligent systems that can augment human intelligence, enhance decision-making, and facilitate interactions between humans and machines continues to grow. By combining the strengths of AI technologies with human-like cognitive abilities, cognitive computing paves the way for innovative solutions that can transform industries, drive innovation, and improve the quality of life.

Ontology and AI

Ontology, in the context of artificial intelligence, refers to the representation of knowledge about a specific domain in a structured and formalized manner. It defines the concepts, entities, relationships, and rules within a domain to facilitate knowledge sharing, reasoning, and decision-making in AI systems.

Ontologies provide a common vocabulary and taxonomy that enable AI systems to understand, interpret, and reason about the information they process. By organizing knowledge in a structured format, ontologies help AI systems handle ambiguity, infer implicit relationships, and make intelligent decisions based on the available information.

In AI applications, ontologies play a crucial role in various tasks, such as natural language processing, information retrieval, knowledge graphs, and semantic modeling. They assist in capturing domain-specific knowledge, mapping relationships between entities, resolving semantic inconsistencies, and enhancing the accuracy and efficiency of AI algorithms.

By incorporating ontologies into AI systems, developers can build more robust, flexible, and interpretable models that can effectively utilize and reason over complex information. Ontologies contribute to the development of intelligent systems that can mimic human-like cognitive processes, understand context, and draw meaningful insights from data across different domains.

Overall, the integration of ontology and AI enables more advanced and sophisticated applications that harness the power of structured knowledge representation to drive innovation, automation, and intelligence in various fields, ultimately advancing the capabilities and potential of artificial intelligence technologies.

AI Ethics

AI ethics refers to the principles, guidelines, and standards that govern the development, deployment, and use of artificial intelligence technologies in an ethical and responsible manner. As AI systems become more pervasive and powerful, ethical considerations become increasingly important to ensure that these technologies align with societal values, respect human rights, and mitigate potential risks and biases.

Key issues in AI ethics include:

1. *Bias and Fairness: AI systems can inherit biases from the data they are trained on, leading to discriminatory outcomes. Ensuring fairness and equity in AI decision-making is essential to prevent harm and uphold principles of justice.*

2. *Transparency and Explainability: Understanding how AI systems arrive at decisions is crucial for accountability, trust, and regulatory compliance. Transparency and explainability mechanisms are necessary for stakeholders to comprehend and challenge AI outcomes.*

3. *Privacy and Data Protection: AI systems often handle sensitive and personal data, raising concerns about privacy violations and data breaches. Safeguarding user data, ensuring consent, and implementing strong data protection measures are critical in AI applications.*

4. *Accountability and Responsibility: Determining who is responsible for AI decision-making and its consequences is a complex issue. Establishing clear lines of accountability, liability frameworks, and governance structures is essential to address ethical challenges in AI.*

5. *Safety and Security: Ensuring the safety and security of AI systems is paramount to prevent malicious attacks, disruptions, or unintended consequences. Robust cybersecurity measures, risk assessments, and safety protocols are vital to mitigate risks in AI deployments.*

6. *Societal Impact: Understanding the broader societal implications of AI technologies, including job displacement, economic inequality, and social polarization, is necessary to address the ethical considerations and promote inclusive and sustainable development.*

To address these ethical challenges, stakeholders, including researchers, policymakers, industry leaders, and ethicists, collaborate to develop frameworks, guidelines, and regulations that promote ethical AI practices. Initiatives such as the development of AI ethics principles, the establishment of ethical review boards, and the integration of ethics education into AI research and development efforts are crucial to foster responsible AI innovation and deployment. By upholding ethical standards and values in AI development and deployment, we can harness the potential of AI technologies to benefit society and advance human well-being.

Deep Learning in AI

Deep learning is a subset of machine learning that focuses on modeling high-level abstractions in data by using neural networks with many layers, referred to as deep neural networks. Deep learning algorithms attempt to learn multiple levels of representation of the data, with each layer in the neural network transforming the data into a more abstract and complex form.

Deep learning has gained significant attention and popularity in the field of artificial intelligence due to its ability to automatically learn features from data, handle large and complex datasets, and outperform traditional machine learning techniques in various tasks such as image and speech recognition, natural language processing, and reinforcement learning.

Key characteristics of deep learning in AI include:

1. *Neural Networks: Deep learning algorithms are typically implemented using artificial neural networks composed of multiple layers of interconnected nodes (neurons). Each layer processes the input data and learns to extract features representing different levels of abstraction.*

2. *Representation Learning: Deep learning focuses on learning representations of data through successive layers of transformations. As the data passes through the layers, the neural network automatically learns to extract relevant features from the input data.*

3. *Training with Back propagation: Deep neural networks are trained using backpropagation, a process that involves computing the gradient of the error and updating the network's parameters to minimize the error between the predicted output and the actual output.*

4. *Deep Convolutional Networks: Convolutional neural networks (CNNs) are a type of deep neural network commonly used in image recognition tasks. CNNs leverage the spatial structure of images through convolutional layers, pooling layers, and fully connected layers to extract features and make predictions.*

5. *Recurrent Neural Networks: Recurrent neural networks (RNNs) are another type of deep learning architecture that can handle sequential data, such as text and time series. RNNs have connections that form loops, allowing them to maintain memory of previous inputs and capture temporal dependencies.*

Deep learning has revolutionized AI applications by enabling machines to learn complex patterns and representations directly from data, without the need for manual feature engineering. Advances in deep learning, coupled with the availability of large datasets and powerful hardware, have driven progress in various domains, leading to breakthroughs in image and speech recognition, natural language understanding, autonomous systems, and more.

As deep learning continues to evolve, researchers are exploring new architectures, optimization techniques, and applications to further enhance the capabilities of AI systems and unlock their potential for solving complex problems and driving innovation in diverse fields.

Neural Networks

Neural networks are a fundamental component of artificial intelligence and machine learning that are inspired by the structure and function of the human brain. They are computational models composed of interconnected nodes, called neurons, organized in layers. Neural networks are designed to learn patterns and relationships in data by adjusting their weights and biases through a process known as training.

Key concepts and components of neural networks include:

1. *Neurons: Neurons are the basic computational units in a neural network. Each neuron receives inputs, applies a transformation using weights and*

biases, and produces an output using an activation function. Neurons in one layer are connected to neurons in the next layer, forming a network.

2. *Layers: Neural networks are typically organized into layers, consisting of an input layer, one or more hidden layers, and an output layer. The input layer receives data, the hidden layers process the data through transformations, and the output layer produces the final predictions or classifications.*

3. *Weights and Biases: The weights and biases in a neural network are parameters that are learned during the training process. They control the strength of connections between neurons and determine how input signals are transformed as they pass through the network.*

4. *Activation Functions: Activation functions introduce non-linearities into the neural network, allowing it to model complex relationships in data. Common activation functions include sigmoid, tanh, ReLU (Rectified Linear Unit), and softmax functions.*

5. *Feedforward and Backpropagation: In a feedforward neural network, data flows through the network from the input layer to the output layer. Backpropagation is an algorithm used to train neural networks by adjusting the weights and biases based on the calculated error between the predicted output and the actual output.*

6. *Deep Neural Networks: Deep neural networks refer to neural networks with multiple hidden layers, enabling them to learn complex patterns and hierarchies of features in data. Deep learning architectures, such as convolutional neural networks (CNNs) and recurrent neural networks (RNNs), leverage deep neural networks for tasks like image recognition and sequence modeling.*

Neural networks have demonstrated remarkable capabilities in various machine learning tasks, including image and speech recognition, natural language processing, recommendation systems, and more. Their ability to learn representations of data and generalize to new examples makes them powerful tools for solving complex problems and developing intelligent systems.

As research in neural networks continues to advance, novel architectures, optimization techniques, and training algorithms are being developed to improve network performance, scalability, and interpretability. Neural networks remain a cornerstone of modern AI technologies, driving innovation and enabling the development of sophisticated solutions across a wide range of applications.

End of Chat GTP's response to Artificial Awareness words and phrases.

Space Force

Secrets of the Space Force

As an AI assistant, I don't have access to classified information or secrets related to the Space Force or any other governmental or military organization. The United States Space Force is a branch of the U.S. Armed Forces responsible for space operations and ensuring the security and defense of U.S. interests in space. While there may be ongoing projects, initiatives, or developments within the Space Force that are not publicly disclosed for security reasons, it is important to respect the confidentiality and national security of such information.

If you have any questions about the Space Force or space-related topics that are publicly available, I would be happy to provide information and insights to the best of my knowledge. Feel free to ask about any non-classified aspects of the Space Force or space exploration, and I'll do my best to assist you!

+What is the Objective of the Space Force

The United States Space Force, established as the sixth branch of the U.S. Armed Forces in December 2019, has several primary objectives focused on ensuring U.S. superiority in space operations and protecting national interests in the space domain. Some key objectives of the Space Force include:

1. *Space Superiority: The Space Force aims to maintain U.S. dominance in space by developing, acquiring, and operating space capabilities that support national security objectives. This includes protecting U.S. space assets, such as satellites, from threats and ensuring freedom of action in space.*

2. *Space Operations: The Space Force is responsible for organizing, training, and equipping space forces to conduct a wide range of space-related operations, including satellite communications, missile warning systems, surveillance, and navigation services.*

3. *National Security: Protecting U.S. national security interests in space is a critical mission of the Space Force. This involves monitoring and responding to potential threats in space, such as anti-satellite weapons, cyber attacks, and other hostile actions that could impact U.S. space capabilities.*

4. *Space Awareness: The Space Force is tasked with improving situational awareness in space by tracking and monitoring objects in orbit, providing early warning of potential hazards, and ensuring the safety and security of space operations.*

5. *International Partnerships: The Space Force collaborates with international allies and partners to promote peaceful and responsible behavior in space, strengthen space cooperation, and enhance space domain awareness through information sharing and joint activities.*

6. *Innovation and Technology Development: To maintain its technological edge in space, the Space Force invests in research, development, and innovation to advance space capabilities, enhance resilience, and address emerging challenges in the space domain.*

Overall, the primary objective of the U.S. Space Force is to protect U.S. interests in space, ensure the security and sustainability of space operations, and maintain leadership in space capabilities to support national security and defense priorities. By focusing on space superiority, operations, security, awareness, international partnerships, and innovation, the Space Force plays a critical role in safeguarding U.S. interests in the increasingly contested and congested space environment.

+How Large in Personnel in the Space Force

As of 2021, the United States Space Force, the newest branch of the U.S. Armed Forces, is still in the process of building its personnel size and organizational structure. The Space Force was officially established in December 2019 with the goal of consolidating and coordinating space-related operations within the military.

The exact number of personnel in the Space Force may vary over time as the branch continues to grow and expand its workforce. While specific figures may not be readily available due to the dynamic nature of military personnel assignments and deployments, the Space Force is comprised of a combination of active-duty military personnel, civilian professionals, and possibly members transitioning from other branches of the military.

The Space Force's focus on space-related operations, technological expertise, and specialized training for space missions requires a workforce with diverse skill sets in areas such as space operations, satellite communications, missile warning systems, cybersecurity, intelligence, engineering, and more.

As the Space Force continues to evolve and establish its presence in the U.S. military landscape, it is expected to grow in size and capabilities with the recruitment and training of personnel dedicated to space operations, national security in space, and advancing U.S. interests in the space domain. The Space Force's personnel numbers and structure will likely continue to develop in the coming years to support its mission objectives and operational requirements in this critical and evolving domain.

American UFOs

Unidentified Flying Objects (UFOs) have been a topic of interest and speculation for decades, with reported sightings and encounters sparking curiosity and debate about the possibility of extraterrestrial life and advanced aerial phenomena. The U.S. government and military have investigated UFO reports over the years, and in recent times, there has been increased public awareness and discussion around unidentified aerial phenomena (UAPs) or "American UFOs."

In 2020, the U.S. Department of Defense established the Unidentified Aerial Phenomena Task Force to investigate and assess UAP sightings reported by military personnel and the general public. The task force aims to gather and analyze data on UAP sightings to determine if these phenomena pose any potential threats to national security or if they can be explained by known sources.

In June 2021, the Office of the Director of National Intelligence released a report to Congress on UAPs, providing a summary of UAP sightings and acknowledging that some of these aerial phenomena remain unexplained. The report highlighted the need for further investigation and research to better understand the nature and origin of UAPs.

It's important to note that while some UFO sightings have been attributed to natural phenomena, weather events, human-made objects, or misidentifications, there are cases that continue to defy conventional explanations. The study of UFOs and UAPs involves a complex and multidisciplinary approach, encompassing scientific analysis, data collection, witness testimonies, and collaboration between governmental agencies, research organizations, and academia.

As interest in UFOs and UAPs persists, ongoing efforts to study and analyze these phenomena with a scientific and evidence-based approach are crucial to advancing our understanding of the unexplained aerial sightings and potentially uncovering new insights about the mysteries of the universe. Whether these sightings have earthly or extraterrestrial origins, the investigation of UFOs and UAPs remains a fascinating and important area of research that captures the imagination of people around the world.

To Catch an Alien

"To Catch an Alien" sounds like an intriguing concept that could be explored in various forms of entertainment, such as books, films, TV shows, or games. The idea of capturing or encountering an alien being raises questions about

interspecies communication, ethical considerations, scientific exploration, and potentially even interstellar diplomacy.

In a fictional context, a story titled "To Catch an Alien" could follow a group of scientists, explorers, or government agents who discover evidence of extraterrestrial life and embark on a mission to interact with or capture an alien entity for study. This narrative could delve into themes of curiosity, the unknown, the search for truth, and the challenges of bridging the gap between humans and beings from another world.

The storyline could involve elements of mystery, suspense, and discovery as the characters navigate encounters with alien technology, behaviors, and environments. Ethical dilemmas may arise regarding the treatment of alien life forms, the consequences of interplanetary contact, and the implications for humanity's place in the universe.

During the journey to catch an alien, the characters could face obstacles, conflicts, and moral choices that shape their understanding of the alien being and their own beliefs about life beyond Earth. The narrative could offer a thought-provoking exploration of what it means to encounter the unknown and how such encounters could impact individuals, societies, and the future of humanity's relationship with the cosmos.

Overall, "To Catch an Alien" has the potential to be a compelling and captivating story that invites audiences to ponder the possibilities of alien life, the mysteries of the universe, and the profound implications of contact with beings from distant worlds. Whether in a work of fiction or as a thought experiment, the idea of catching an alien sparks imagination, wonder, and a sense of adventure in exploring the boundaries of what lies beyond our planet.

<u>How to Stop an Assassination</u>

Preventing or stopping an assassination is a complex and serious matter that requires careful planning, coordination, and risk management. If you believe there is a threat of an assassination attempt, here are some general steps that could be taken to enhance security and reduce the risk:

1. ***Security Assessment**: Conduct a thorough security assessment to identify potential vulnerabilities and threats. Evaluate the individual or location that may be targeted for an assassination attempt.*

2. ***Increased Security Measures**: Enhance physical security measures, such as increasing the number of security personnel, implementing access controls, installing surveillance systems, and conducting regular security patrols.*

3. ***Risk Mitigation Strategies**: Develop risk mitigation strategies based on the specific threat assessment. This could include implementing protective measures, changing routines, and establishing emergency response plans.*

4. ***Intelligence Gathering**: Collect intelligence on potential threats and individuals or groups that may be planning the assassination. Stay vigilant and monitor for any suspicious activities or behavior.*

5. ***Security Briefings**: Provide security briefings to individuals at risk of being targeted for assassination. Educate them on personal safety measures, threat awareness, and emergency response protocols.*

6. ***Collaboration with Law Enforcement**: Work closely with law enforcement agencies to share threat information, coordinate security efforts, and seek assistance in preventing any potential attacks.*

7. **Communication Protocols**: Establish communication protocols for reporting suspicious activities, threats, or security incidents. Encourage individuals to report any concerning behavior promptly.

8. **Training and Drills**: Conduct security training sessions and emergency drills to prepare individuals for responding to potential threats, attacks, or emergencies effectively.

9. **Public Awareness**: If the threat of an assassination is high-profile, consider increasing public awareness and communication about the potential risks and security measures in place to protect individuals.

10. **Seek Professional Assistance**: In cases of credible threats or imminent danger, consider seeking assistance from professional security consultants, threat assessment experts, or law enforcement agencies with expertise in protective services.

It's important to note that every situation is unique, and the specific measures taken to stop an assassination will depend on the nature of the threat, the individuals involved, and the resources available. Prioritizing security, threat assessment, communication, and proactive prevention strategies are key to mitigating risks and ensuring the safety of individuals at risk of being targeted for an assassination.

Iron Man Army

The concept of an Iron Man army could involve the development and deployment of a fleet of advanced robotic suits or exoskeletons inspired by the iconic Iron Man suit from the Marvel Universe. These suits could be designed to enhance the capabilities of military forces, law enforcement agencies, or emergency responders in various operational scenarios.

Here are some potential features and applications of an Iron Man army:

1. **Enhanced Strength and Mobility**: *The suits could provide wearers with superhuman strength, agility, and speed, enabling them to perform physically demanding tasks and maneuvers with ease.*

2. **Integrated Weapons Systems**: *Equipped with advanced weaponry such as repulsors, missiles, energy blasters, and other high-tech armaments, the suits could be formidable combat units on the battlefield.*

3. **Advanced Sensors and Targeting Systems**: *Built-in sensors, targeting systems, and heads-up displays could enhance situational awareness, accuracy, and decision-making for users during missions.*

4. **Durability and Protection**: *The suits could be armored with advanced materials capable of withstanding ballistic, energy-based, and environmental threats to protect users from harm.*

5. **Flight Capabilities**: *Some iterations of the Iron Man army suits could feature flight systems, allowing wearers to navigate and engage targets from the air.*

6. **Medical and Emergency Response Features**: *Incorporating medical sensors, communication systems, and life-saving capabilities could make the suits valuable assets for search and rescue missions, disaster response efforts, and medical evacuations.*

7. **Customization and Adaptability**: *Modular design elements and customization options could allow users to tailor the suits to their specific needs and preferences for different mission profiles.*

While the concept of an Iron Man army offers exciting possibilities for enhancing operational capabilities and protecting personnel in challenging environments, it also raises ethical, legal, and strategic considerations. Questions about control, oversight, autonomy, accountability, and the impact of advanced technology on warfare would need to be carefully addressed when designing and deploying such systems.

Ultimately, the development of an Iron Man army would require extensive research, development, testing, and evaluation to ensure the effectiveness, safety, and ethical use of these advanced technologies in support of national security, public safety, and humanitarian efforts.

Nightstalkers

The Nightstalkers are a fictional organization that has appeared in various forms of media, including movies, television shows, comic books, and video games. In different contexts, the Nightstalkers may refer to different groups or individuals with specific roles and characteristics. One notable depiction of the Nightstalkers is in the Marvel Comics universe, where they are a team of supernatural specialists who hunt vampires and other mystical threats.

In the 1998 film "Blade: Trinity," the Nightstalkers are a group of vampire hunters led by Hannibal King, Abigail Whistler, and the legendary vampire hunter Blade. The Nightstalkers use advanced weapons, technology, and combat skills to battle vampires and other supernatural creatures in an ongoing struggle to protect humanity from the forces of darkness.

In military terminology, Night Stalkers may refer to the 160th Special Operations Aviation Regiment (Airborne), a U.S. Army special operations unit known for conducting nighttime missions, often involving helicopter-based operations in support of special operations forces.

Overall, whether in fiction or reality, the name Nightstalkers carries connotations of darkness, stealth, specialization, and a willingness to confront threats in the shadows. The concept of night operations, clandestine missions, and facing formidable adversaries under cover of darkness adds intrigue and mystery to the persona of the Nightstalkers across different storytelling mediums.

"This seems to be quite useful," said Ashley. "Some of the information is superfluous but I would say that represents life in general."

"The plus sign just before a query denotes that it is a subset, of the original query," said Matt. "Logically, one should class all of the information together."

Robots

Future Robotic Warfare

The future of robotic warfare presents a complex landscape shaped by advances in technology, ethical considerations, international regulations, and strategic implications. As robotic systems continue to evolve and become more sophisticated, they are likely to play an increasingly significant role in modern warfare. Here are some key aspects to consider regarding future robotic warfare:

1. ***Autonomous Systems***: *Autonomous robots and drones equipped with artificial intelligence could be deployed for a range of military applications, including reconnaissance, surveillance, target acquisition, and even decision-making in combat situations. The development of fully autonomous weapons raises ethical questions about accountability, human control, and the potential for unintended consequences.*

2.   **Swarm Robotics**: Swarm robotics involves coordinating multiple robots to work together towards a common goal. In a military context, swarm robots could be used for tasks such as surveillance, search and rescue missions, or even coordinated attacks on enemy targets. The ability to deploy swarms of robots could provide a tactical advantage on the battlefield.

3.   **Unmanned Aerial Vehicles (UAVs)**: Drones have already become a prominent feature of modern warfare, offering capabilities for intelligence, surveillance, reconnaissance, and precision strikes. Future UAVs may feature advanced stealth, endurance, speed, and autonomous operation, transforming the nature of aerial warfare.

4.   **Ground Robotics**: Ground robots could be used for tasks such as logistics support, demining operations, patrolling, and combat roles on the battlefield. These robots could enhance

Secrets of the Paranormal

The paranormal is a realm of mysterious phenomena and unexplained experiences that fascinate and intrigue many individuals. While the secrets of the paranormal remain elusive and often defy scientific explanation, there are several key themes and concepts often associated with this field:

1.   **Ghosts**: One of the most well-known aspects of the paranormal, ghosts are believed to be spirits or entities of the dead that linger in the physical world. Reports of ghostly apparitions, unexplained noises, and strange occurrences in supposedly haunted locations have fueled interest in ghost hunting and paranormal investigation.

2.   **UFOs and Extraterrestrial Life**: Unidentified Flying Objects (UFOs) and claims of encounters with extraterrestrial beings have

long captured the public imagination. The search for evidence of alien visitations, government cover-ups, and the existence of intelligent life beyond Earth continues to be a topic of debate and speculation.

3. **Psychic Abilities**: Psychic phenomena, such as telepathy, clairvoyance, precognition, and psychokinesis, suggest the existence of capabilities that transcend conventional scientific understanding. Individuals claiming psychic abilities have been studied and researched to explore the potential of extrasensory perception.

4. **Cryptids and Monsters**: Cryptids are creatures of folklore and legend that are said to exist but have not been scientifically proven. Examples include Bigfoot, the Loch Ness Monster, and the Chupacabra. Sightings and encounters with these mysterious beings fuel interest in cryptozoology and the search for undiscovered species.

5. **Parapsychology**: Parapsychology is the study of paranormal phenomena using scientific methods. Researchers in this field investigate topics such as telepathy, psychokinesis, near-death experiences, and hauntings, seeking to understand the nature of these phenomena and their potential implications for our understanding of consciousness and reality.

6. **Ancient Mysteries**: The paranormal is often intertwined with ancient mysteries, such as lost civilizations, archaeological enigmas, and unexplained phenomena from the distant past. The exploration of ancient sites, artifacts, and texts can offer insights into the unexplained and the supernatural.

While the paranormal remains a realm of speculation, belief, and mystery, it continues to spark curiosity and inspire exploration into the unknown. The search for answers and the quest to unravel the secrets of the paranormal reflect humanity's enduring fascination with the unexplained and the supernatural.

HARRY KATZAN JR.

Secret World of Mind control

The concept of mind control, also known as brainwashing or thought manipulation, has long been a subject of intrigue and speculation in popular culture, psychology, and conspiracy theories. The idea of influencing or controlling someone's thoughts, beliefs, and behaviors without their consent raises ethical, psychological, and philosophical questions about the nature of free will and autonomy. Here are some key aspects of the secret world of mind control:

1. **Historical Context**: *Mind control techniques have been explored and employed throughout history, often in the context of warfare, espionage, cults, and propaganda. Methods such as psychological manipulation, hypnosis, drugs, and coercive persuasion have been used to influence individuals and groups for various purposes.*

2. **Psychological Manipulation**: *Psychological techniques, such as gaslighting, persuasion, and emotional manipulation, can be used to exert control over someone's thoughts and behaviors. Cults, abusive relationships, and authoritarian regimes are known to employ tactics that undermine an individual's sense of reality and agency.*

3. **Subliminal Messaging**: *The use of subliminal messages, hidden cues, and suggestive imagery in media and advertising has raised concerns about the potential for subconscious influence on people's preferences, attitudes, and behaviors. The effectiveness and ethics of subliminal messaging remain topics of debate among psychologists and media experts.*

4. **Cognitive Control**: *Advances in neuroscience and cognitive science have led to research on techniques for modulating cognitive functions and influencing decision-making processes. Brain stimulation, neurofeedback, and cognitive enhancement technologies raise questions*

138

about the boundaries of ethical behavior and the potential for unintended consequences.

5. **Conspiracy Theories**: *The idea of secret government programs, covert organizations, and clandestine experiments involving mind control has given rise to numerous conspiracy theories. Stories of alleged mind control experiments, such as the CIA's MKUltra program, spark debate and speculation about the extent of human manipulation.*

6. **Ethical Considerations**: *The ethical implications of mind control raise profound questions about privacy, consent, autonomy, and the limits of psychological influence. Safeguarding individual rights, promoting informed consent, and upholding ethical standards in research and practice are essential in addressing concerns related to mind control.*

While the secret world of mind control remains shrouded in mystery and controversy, exploring the ethical, psychological, and societal dimensions of influence and persuasion can deepen our understanding of human behavior and the complexities of cognitive manipulation. Understanding the mechanisms of mind control and its implications can help individuals recognize and resist undue influence while promoting transparency, critical thinking, and ethical decision-making.

Presidential Power Secrets

The exercise of presidential power is a complex and multifaceted aspect of government that involves a combination of constitutional authority, political influence, institutional norms, and public perception. While some aspects of presidential power are enshrined in the Constitution, there are also certain nuances, practices, and strategies that can be considered "secrets" of presidential power. Here are some key insights into the exercise of presidential power:

1.   **Executive Orders**: *One of the lesser-known "secrets" of presidential power is the use of executive orders, which allow the president to dictate policy without congressional approval. Executive orders can be a powerful tool for shaping domestic and foreign policy, bypassing legislative gridlock, and responding quickly to emergent issues.*

2.   **National Security Directives**: *National Security Presidential Memoranda (NSPMs) and National Security Council Directives (NSCDs) are classified documents that outline the president's decisions and directives on national security matters. These documents play a crucial role in shaping the administration's security and foreign policy strategies.*

3.   **Political Appointments**: *The president's power to appoint individuals to key positions within the executive branch, including cabinet members, judges, and agency heads, can have a significant impact on policy implementation and decision-making. Leveraging these appointments strategically can influence the direction of government operations.*

4.   **Informal Powers**: *Informal powers, such as the president's ability to set the policy agenda, shape public opinion, and engage in diplomatic initiatives, can have a profound impact on the exercise of presidential power. These informal tools of influence often complement formal constitutional powers.*

5.   **Presidential Communication**: *Effective communication strategies, including public speeches, press conferences, social media, and other forms of outreach, are essential for conveying the president's priorities, goals, and initiatives to the public and shaping public perception.*

6.   **Presidential Pardons**: *The president's power to grant pardons and commutations can be a secretive and powerful tool for exercising executive*

clemency, influencing legal outcomes, and shaping perceptions of justice and mercy.

While the exercise of presidential power is subject to checks and balances from other branches of government, the president's ability to wield formal and informal tools of influence can shape policy outcomes, public opinion, and the direction of the nation. Understanding the complexities and nuances of presidential power can provide insights into the dynamics of governance and the exercise of authority in a democratic society.

USS Jimmy Carter

The USS Jimmy Carter (SSN-23) is a U.S. Navy Seawolf-class nuclear-powered submarine. It is named after the 39th President of the United States, Jimmy Carter. Commissioned in 2005, the USS Jimmy Carter is known for its unique modifications and capabilities, which have led to speculation about its special missions and operations.

One of the most notable features of the USS Jimmy Carter is its extended hull section, known as the Multi-Mission Platform (MMP). This section provides additional space for a variety of missions, including intelligence gathering, underwater operations, and special forces deployments. The submarine's enhanced flexibility and versatility make it well-suited for classified missions and strategic activities.

Given its advanced technology and secretive nature, the USS Jimmy Carter has attracted curiosity and speculation about its potential roles and missions, leading to its reputation as a highly specialized and secretive asset within the U.S. Navy's submarine fleet.

Secret Paranormal Research

The world of secret paranormal research is a realm shrouded in mystery and intrigue, often involving investigations into phenomena beyond the scope of conventional science. This clandestine field may encompass a variety of activities, including the study of ghosts, UFOs, cryptids, psychic abilities, and other mysterious occurrences.

In this obscure world of supernatural inquiry, researchers might delve into haunted locations, conduct experiments to test psychic phenomena, analyze unexplained sightings, and explore ancient legends and myths. The secrecy surrounding these investigations could be attributed to the potential consequences of revealing information that challenges mainstream beliefs or poses unexplained phenomena.

Secret paranormal research may involve collaboration with government agencies, private organizations, or independent researchers with specialized knowledge in the supernatural. The goal of such research could be to unlock the secrets of the unexplained, uncover hidden truths about the nature of reality, or even harness paranormal phenomena for various purposes.

While the existence of covert paranormal research projects remains largely speculative, the allure of the unknown and the possibility of unlocking the mysteries of the supernatural continue to captivate the imagination of those who venture into this enigmatic realm of exploration and discovery.

Secrets of Drone Warfare

Drone warfare, also known as unmanned aerial vehicle (UAV) warfare, has revolutionized modern military operations, offering both advantages and ethical challenges. Here are some of the key aspects and secrets surrounding drone warfare:

1. **Precision and Targeted Strikes**: One of the main advantages of drone warfare is the ability to conduct precise and targeted strikes against enemy targets, minimizing collateral damage compared to traditional methods of warfare.

2. **Surveillance and Reconnaissance**: Drones are used extensively for surveillance and reconnaissance missions, providing real-time intelligence to military forces. This enables commanders to make informed decisions and better plan military operations.

3. **Secret Missions and Covert Operations**: Drones are often used in secret missions and covert operations to gather intelligence, track high-value targets, and conduct airstrikes without direct engagement of ground forces.

4. **Remote Piloting**: Drone operators can control the aircraft from a remote location, often thousands of miles away from the actual battlefield. This enables 24/7 surveillance and strike capabilities, but also raises ethical concerns about the detachment of warfare from the human experience.

5. **Legal and Ethical Challenges**: Drone warfare has sparked debates about its legality, ethical implications, and risks of civilian casualties. The secrecy surrounding drone operations can sometimes lead to accountability issues and questions about transparency.

6. **Advancements in Technology**: The development of artificial intelligence, machine learning, and autonomous drones is shaping the future of drone warfare, potentially raising concerns about the implications of autonomous weapons systems.

While drone warfare offers strategic advantages in modern military operations, the secrecy surrounding its use, the ethical dilemmas it raises, and the potential for unintended consequences highlight the need for careful consideration and scrutiny of this evolving form of warfare.

Terrorism and Criminals

Tracking Terror: The 9/11 Plot

The 9/11 terrorist attacks, which occurred on September 11, 2001, were a series of coordinated suicide attacks carried out by the extremist group al-Qaeda against the United States. Here are some key points about the 9/11 plot:

1. ***Planning and Coordination**: The 9/11 attacks were meticulously planned and coordinated by al-Qaeda operatives, with the mastermind identified as Khalid Sheikh Mohammed. The attackers were trained in flying commercial aircraft and carried out the attacks with precision.*

2. ***Terrorist Hijackings**: On the morning of September 11, 2001, 19 hijackers took control of four commercial airplanes. They intentionally crashed two planes into the World Trade Center towers in New York City, one into the Pentagon in Arlington, Virginia, and the fourth plane, United Airlines Flight 93, crashed in a field in Pennsylvania after passengers attempted to overcome the hijackers.*

3. ***Casualties and Impact**: The 9/11 attacks resulted in the deaths of nearly 3,000 people and caused significant destruction and devastation. The attacks had far-reaching consequences, leading to a global war on terror, changes in U.S. national security policies, and increased vigilance in counterterrorism efforts worldwide.*

4.   **Investigations and Aftermath**: Following the attacks, extensive investigations were conducted to identify the perpetrators, accomplices, and sources of support. The U.S. government launched military campaigns in Afghanistan and later in Iraq as part of the response to the attacks.

5.   **Legacy and Remembrance**: The 9/11 attacks left a lasting impact on the United States and the world, shaping policies on national security, counterterrorism, surveillance, and immigration. The day is commemorated annually as a national day of remembrance and serves as a reminder of the resilience and unity in the face of tragedy.

The 9/11 plot stands as a tragic chapter in global history, underscoring the persistent threat of terrorism and the importance of international cooperation in combating extremist ideologies and enhancing security measures to prevent future attacks.

The Norte Valle Cartel

The Norte Valley Cartel is a fictional criminal organization often depicted in movies, TV shows, books, and other forms of entertainment. While not based on a real criminal group, the Norte Valley Cartel is typically portrayed as a powerful and ruthless drug cartel operating in a fictional region, blending elements of organized crime, corruption, violence, and intrigue.

In fictional depictions, the Norte Valley Cartel is often characterized by its control of the drug trade, financial resources, influence over local authorities, and willingness to resort to extreme measures to protect its interests and maintain dominance in the criminal underworld. Stories involving the Norte Valley Cartel may explore themes such as loyalty, betrayal, power struggles, and the human cost of involvement in illicit activities.

The portrayal of the Norte Valley Cartel in fiction serves to create compelling narratives, explore complex characters, and engage audiences with thrilling and suspenseful storylines. While not a real criminal organization, the Norte Valley Cartel exemplifies the fascination with crime dramas and the exploration of the darker aspects of human nature in storytelling.

The Terrorist Next Door: Operation Smokescreen

"Operation Smokescreen" is a hypothetical scenario involving a fictional terrorist plot orchestrated by a shadowy extremist group with connections to domestic terrorism. In this fictional narrative, the terrorist organization operates covertly within a community, blending in with everyday life while secretly planning and preparing for a major attack.

Key elements of "Operation Smokescreen" might include:

1. **Infiltration and Radicalization**: *The terrorist group infiltrates the community, recruiting and radicalizing individuals to carry out their deadly mission. Members of the group may appear as ordinary neighbors, coworkers, or acquaintances, hiding their true intentions behind a facade of normalcy.*

2. **Covert Planning and Preparation**: *The terrorists carefully plan and prepare for their attack, using encrypted communications, safe houses, and anonymous funding sources to avoid detection by authorities. They may acquire weapons, explosives, and logistics while operating under the radar.*

3. **Surveillance and Reconnaissance**: *The terrorists conduct surveillance on potential targets, gathering intelligence and assessing vulnerabilities to maximize the impact of their attack. They may monitor security*

measures, patterns of life, and response times of authorities to exploit weaknesses in the system.

4. **False Flags and Misdirection**: As part of "Operation Smokescreen," the terrorists may deploy tactics of misinformation, false flags, and misdirection to confuse law enforcement agencies and divert attention away from their true intentions. By sowing confusion and chaos, they aim to create cover for their nefarious activities.

5. **Counterterrorism Response**: Law enforcement and intelligence agencies, in collaboration with community members, work tirelessly to uncover the terrorist plot, disrupt the operation, and prevent the attack. Through surveillance, intelligence analysis, and coordinated efforts, they strive to bring the terrorists to justice and prevent loss of life.

"Operation Smokescreen" serves as a fictional narrative that explores the themes of terrorism, national security, community resilience, and the complexities of combating violent extremism. By delving into the hypothetical scenario of a terrorist threat emerging from within a community, this storyline underscores the importance of vigilance, cooperation, and preparedness in safeguarding against acts of terrorism.

Hunting War Criminals

Hunting war criminals is a challenging and complex task that involves international cooperation, legal frameworks, intelligence gathering, and dedicated efforts by law enforcement agencies and international tribunals. Here are some key aspects of hunting war criminals:

1. **Identification and Investigation**: The first step in hunting war criminals is to identify individuals suspected of committing war crimes, crimes against humanity, or genocide. This often involves collecting

evidence, conducting interviews, and analyzing testimonies to build cases against perpetrators.

2. **International Tribunals**: *International bodies such as the International Criminal Court (ICC), the International Criminal Tribunal for the former Yugoslavia (ICTY), and the International Criminal Tribunal for Rwanda (ICTR) play a crucial role in prosecuting war criminals and holding them accountable for their actions.*

3. **National Jurisdictions**: *National courts and legal systems also have a responsibility to prosecute war criminals under the principle of universal jurisdiction, allowing countries to prosecute individuals for serious crimes regardless of where the crimes were committed.*

4. **Cooperation and Extradition**: *Hunting war criminals often requires international cooperation, extradition treaties, and diplomatic efforts to apprehend suspects and transfer them to the appropriate jurisdiction for prosecution. This can be a lengthy and complex process, especially when suspects are located in different countries.*

5. **Intelligence and Surveillance**: *Law enforcement agencies and intelligence services use advanced technologies, surveillance methods, and investigative techniques to track down war criminals who may be hiding in remote locations or using false identities to evade capture.*

6. **Public Awareness and Advocacy**: *Public awareness campaigns, advocacy efforts, and grassroots movements play a vital role in raising awareness about war crimes, promoting justice for victims, and pressuring governments to prioritize the apprehension and prosecution of war criminals.*

Hunting war criminals is a critical aspect of upholding international humanitarian law, seeking justice for victims of atrocities, and deterring future crimes against humanity. By pursuing accountability for those responsible for war crimes, the international community sends a powerful message that impunity will not be tolerated, and that perpetrators will be held accountable for their actions.

The Spy Game: Russian Espionage

Russian espionage has a long and storied history, dating back to the days of the Soviet Union and continuing into the present day. Russian intelligence agencies, such as the Foreign Intelligence Service (SVR) and the Main Intelligence Directorate (GRU), are known for their sophisticated and aggressive espionage operations around the world.

Here are some key aspects of Russian espionage:

1. ***Historical Context**: Russian espionage has deep roots in history, with the Soviet era marked by the activities of infamous intelligence agencies like the KGB. Cold War espionage between the Soviet Union and the United States was characterized by high-stakes operations, double agents, and deep cover spies.*

2. ***Modern Operations**: Russian espionage continues to be a significant concern for Western intelligence agencies. The SVR and the GRU are known for their activities in gathering intelligence, conducting cyber operations, and engaging in covert influence campaigns to further Russia's strategic interests.*

3. ***Cyber Espionage**: Russia is known for its advanced capabilities in cyber espionage, including hacking, disinformation campaigns, and online influence operations. Russian hackers have been linked to cyber*

attacks on government agencies, businesses, and critical infrastructure in various countries.

4. **Illegals Program**: The "Illegals Program," as famously portrayed in the TV series "The Americans," involved Russian spies operating under deep cover in foreign countries, assuming false identities and blending into society to gather intelligence and carry out covert operations.

5. **Espionage Tradecraft**: Russian spies are trained in a range of espionage tradecraft, including surveillance, covert communication methods, document forgery, and psychological manipulation. They are skilled in the art of espionage and deception, using a combination of technology and human intelligence to achieve their objectives.

6. **Counterintelligence Efforts**: Western intelligence agencies, such as the CIA, MI6, and European counterparts, actively monitor and counter Russian espionage activities through surveillance, intelligence analysis, and efforts to disrupt and deter Russian intelligence operations.

Russian espionage remains a significant aspect of global security threats, with ongoing concerns about Russian interference in elections, cyber attacks, and intelligence gathering activities. Understanding the tactics, capabilities, and motivations of Russian intelligence agencies is crucial for defending against and countering the threats posed by Russian espionage.

Buried Secrets: Unbreakable Codes

"Buried Secrets: Unbreakable Codes" suggests a compelling narrative involving hidden messages, cryptic communications, and the challenge of cracking seemingly unbreakable codes. This fictional storyline could explore the world of cryptography, espionage, and intrigue, weaving together themes of mystery, deception, and the quest for hidden knowledge.

In this hypothetical scenario, "Buried Secrets" could center around a cryptic message or encoded information that holds the key to a long-buried secret or valuable treasure. The protagonist, perhaps a skilled cryptographer or codebreaker, becomes entangled in a web of deception as they race against time to decipher the unbreakable code and unravel the mystery.

Key elements of the storyline could include:

1. ***The Cryptic Message**: The story kicks off with the discovery of a cryptic message, encrypted using a sophisticated and seemingly unbreakable code. The message hints at a hidden treasure, a dangerous conspiracy, or a long-forgotten secret that could change everything.*

2. ***The Codebreaker**: The protagonist, a brilliant codebreaker with a knack for unraveling complex ciphers, is recruited to decipher the mysterious code. Armed with their expertise in cryptography and a keen eye for patterns, the codebreaker delves into the intricate world of encryption to crack the code and reveal its secrets.*

3. ***Espionage and Intrigue**: As the codebreaker delves deeper into the encrypted message, they attract the attention of shadowy figures, rival cryptographers, and perhaps even intelligence agencies vying to control the valuable information hidden within the code. The stakes are high, and danger lurks around every corner.*

4. ***Decoding the Mystery**: Through a series of twists and turns, the codebreaker follows a trail of clues, breaks through layers of encryption, and uncovers the truth behind the cryptic message. The race against time intensifies as enemies close in, leading to a climactic showdown that could change the course of history.*

5.   **Themes of Trust and Betrayal**: Along the way, the codebreaker must navigate a web of deception, betrayal, and shifting alliances as they seek to unlock the secrets hidden within the unbreakable code. Who can be trusted, and who is working against them in their quest for the truth?

"Buried Secrets: Unbreakable Codes" offers a captivating premise for a thrilling tale of mystery, suspense, and intellectual challenge, blending elements of cryptography, espionage, and high-stakes intrigue. It explores the timeless fascination with hidden messages, unsolved mysteries, and the power of knowledge, inviting audiences to embark on a thrilling journey into the world of codebreaking and discovery.

Additional Subjects

Night Stalkers

"Night Stalkers" conjures up images of stealth, darkness, and danger, suggesting a story filled with intrigue, suspense, and high-octane action. This title could be used for a fictional work that follows a specialized group of elite operatives or a covert tactical unit who operate under the cover of darkness to carry out daring missions and confront formidable enemies.

In this hypothetical scenario, "Night Stalkers" could be a thrilling tale of bravery, sacrifice, and heroism as the team navigates treacherous situations, faces overwhelming odds, and battles against insurmountable challenges. The narrative could explore themes of loyalty, camaraderie, and the human cost of warfare as the Night Stalkers embark on missions that push them to their limits.

Key elements of the storyline could include:

1. **Special Operations**: The Night Stalkers could be a highly trained and specialized unit within the military or a government agency, tasked with executing classified missions that require precision, stealth, and swift action under the cover of darkness.

2. **Dangerous Missions**: The Night Stalkers could be deployed to hotspots around the world to conduct rescue operations, gather intelligence, eliminate high-value targets, or thwart terrorist threats. Their missions could take them into hostile territory, where they must rely on their training, wits, and teamwork to survive.

3. **Intrigue and Betrayal**: As the Night Stalkers face formidable adversaries and navigate complex political landscapes, they may encounter betrayal, deception, and moral dilemmas that test their resolve and question the boundaries of operations.

Night Vision Technology

Night vision technology has revolutionized the way we see and operate in low-light or nighttime environments, enabling enhanced visibility and surveillance capabilities in situations where natural light is limited. This advanced technology amplifies ambient light or infrared radiation, allowing users to see in the dark with clarity and detail that would otherwise be impossible.

In fictional storytelling, "Night Vision Technology" could serve as a compelling theme or plot device to create suspenseful and action-packed scenarios. Here are some ways this theme could be incorporated into a narrative:

1. **Military Thriller**: The story could follow a special operations team equipped with cutting-edge night vision technology on a high-stakes mission behind enemy lines. The use of night vision goggles, scopes,

and thermal imaging devices could add a layer of tension and realism to the action-packed sequences as the team navigates through darkness to achieve their objective.

2. **Survival Adventure**: In a survival or wilderness adventure story, characters could rely on night vision equipment to navigate through a dark and dangerous landscape, evading threats and uncovering hidden dangers as they strive to survive. The juxtaposition of light and shadow could create a visually striking backdrop for the characters' journey.

3. **Mystery or Thriller**: Night vision technology could play a key role in unraveling a mystery or uncovering hidden secrets in a suspenseful narrative. A detective or investigator equipped with night vision gear could piece together clues in the shadows, revealing a clandestine plot or solving a crime that unfolds under the cover of darkness.

4. **Sci-Fi or Futuristic Setting**: Set in a futuristic world, a sci-fi story could explore the implications of advanced night vision technology, perhaps featuring characters with cybernetic enhancements that grant them enhanced vision capabilities in all lighting conditions. This futuristic twist could lead to unique storytelling opportunities and intriguing world-building.

Overall, "Night Vision Technology" presents a versatile and dynamic theme that can add depth, excitement, and intrigue to a wide range of fictional narratives, from military thrillers to sci-fi adventures and beyond. Its ability to illuminate the unseen and unveil hidden truths makes it a compelling element for crafting immersive and engaging stories.

Military Drones

Military drones, also known as unmanned aerial vehicles (UAVs), have revolutionized modern warfare with their capabilities for reconnaissance, surveillance, and targeted strikes. These advanced aerial systems can be operated remotely, providing military forces with valuable intelligence, precision firepower, and strategic advantages on the battlefield.

In fictional storytelling, "Military Drones" could serve as a compelling theme or plot device to explore the ethical, tactical, and political implications of unmanned warfare. Here are some ways this theme could be incorporated into a narrative:

1. ***Political Intrigue**: A fictional story could center around a high-stakes political conflict where military drones play a pivotal role in shaping the outcome. The narrative could delve into debates over the morality of drone warfare, the consequences of remote-controlled attacks, and the complex decision-making processes involved in using these advanced technologies.*

2. ***Technological Thriller**: In a fast-paced thriller, military drones could be hacked or repurposed by rogue actors, leading to a series of escalating crises and high-octane action sequences. The protagonist could be a skilled drone pilot racing against time to prevent a catastrophic attack orchestrated by a shadowy adversary.*

3. ***Human vs. Machine**: The narrative could explore the themes of man versus machine, as characters grapple with the psychological, moral, and emotional implications of using drones in combat. The story could delve into the human cost of remote warfare, as well as the blurred boundaries between autonomy and control in a world where machines make life-and-death decisions.*

4. **Future Warfare**: *Set in a futuristic world, a sci-fi story could imagine a landscape dominated by autonomous military drones, where humans and machines coexist in a complex web of alliances and conflicts. The narrative could explore themes of artificial intelligence, autonomy, and the evolution of warfare in an age of technological advancements.*

Overall, "Military Drones" presents a thought-provoking and timely theme that can add depth, tension, and moral complexity to fictional narratives across genres. Its portrayal of cutting-edge technology, ethical dilemmas, and the changing nature of warfare offers ample storytelling opportunities to explore the intersection of humanity and machines in a world shaped by innovation and conflict.

Hypersonic Unmanned Vehicles

Hypersonic unmanned vehicles represent a cutting-edge technology that combines the high-speed capabilities of hypersonic aircraft with the unmanned, autonomous operation of drones. These advanced vehicles can travel at speeds exceeding Mach 5, allowing for rapid response times, long-range missions, and high maneuverability in both military and civilian applications.

In fictional storytelling, "Hypersonic Unmanned Vehicles" offer a wealth of creative possibilities and narrative intrigue. Here are some ways this concept could be incorporated into a story:

1. **Military Thriller**: *The story could follow a covert military operation centered around a hypersonic unmanned vehicle equipped with advanced weaponry and surveillance capabilities. As the vehicle navigates high-speed missions in hostile territories, the protagonist must grapple with the ethical dilemmas of autonomous warfare and the implications of deploying cutting-edge technology in combat.*

2. **Espionage Adventure**: In a high-stakes espionage narrative, rival intelligence agencies could race to acquire a top-secret hypersonic drone prototype with game-changing capabilities. The fast-paced story could unfold as agents engage in clandestine operations, high-speed chases, and daring heists to secure or sabotage the futuristic technology.

3. **Search and Rescue Drama**: Set in a near-future world, the story could focus on a team of emergency responders utilizing hypersonic unmanned vehicles to conduct rapid search and rescue missions in disaster-stricken areas. The narrative could explore themes of heroism, innovation, and the lifesaving potential of cutting-edge technology in times of crisis.

4. **Space Exploration Saga**: Venturing into the realm of science fiction, the narrative could imagine a future where hypersonic unmanned vehicles are used for interstellar travel,

Skunk Works

The term "Skunk Works" originated from a top-secret research and development facility established by Lockheed Martin in the 1940s. This facility, located in Burbank, California, was responsible for developing cutting-edge aircraft designs, including the iconic U-2 spy plane and the SR-71 Blackbird, among others. The name "Skunk Works" was inspired by the Al Capp comic strip "Li'l Abner," where a fictional moonshine factory was called "Skonk Works."

The Skunk Works team was known for its unconventional approach to innovation, working quickly and collaboratively to tackle complex engineering challenges and deliver groundbreaking aircraft designs. The group operated with a high level of autonomy and secrecy, often pushing the boundaries of technology and engineering to create aircraft that were ahead of their time.

Over the years, the Skunk Works concept has become synonymous with high-performance, cutting-edge technology development in a fast-paced and creative environment. The term is now used more broadly to refer to any innovative and agile project team that operates outside of traditional organizational structures to achieve ambitious goals.

In fiction, "Skunk Works" can evoke themes of innovation, secrecy, expertise, and high-stakes challenges. Stories inspired by the concept of Skunk Works may explore the world of advanced technology, espionage, and unconventional problem-solving in a high-pressure environment. Whether set in the realm of aerospace engineering, military operations, or futuristic worlds, narratives featuring a Skunk Works-like organization can captivate readers with tales of daring innovation, brilliant minds at work, and the thrill of pushing the limits of what is possible.

Project Star

"Project Star" could evoke a sense of grandeur, mystery, and ambition in fictional storytelling. This name suggests a top-secret, high-stakes endeavor that involves astronomical proportions, whether in the realms of science, exploration, or innovation. Here are some ways "Project Star" could be incorporated into a compelling narrative:

1. ***Space Exploration Epic**: "Project Star" could serve as the code name for a groundbreaking mission to explore deep space, discover new planets, or unravel the mysteries of the universe. The story could follow a diverse crew of astronauts, scientists, and engineers as they embark on a perilous journey beyond the stars, encountering cosmic wonders, alien civilizations, and profound revelations along the way.*

2. **Advanced Technology Initiative**: In a near-future world, "Project Star" could represent a cutting-edge research program focused on developing revolutionary technologies for space travel, energy generation, or communication with extraterrestrial life. The narrative could delve into the scientific breakthroughs, ethical dilemmas, and geopolitical tensions surrounding this ambitious project.

3. **Apocalyptic Scenario**: "Project Star" could be the last-ditch effort to save humanity from a cataclysmic event, such as a global pandemic, asteroid impact, or environmental collapse. The story could follow a group of survivors working on the project to build a starship, space colony, or other refuge to ensure the continuation of the human species in the face of impending doom.

4. **Secret Government Experiment**: "Project Star" could be a clandestine government initiative shrouded in conspiracy, intrigue, and danger. The narrative could center on a whistleblower, journalist, or insider seeking to expose the truth behind the project's true purpose, whether it involves advanced weaponry, mind control experiments, or contact with extraterrestrial beings.

Overall, "Project Star" offers a versatile and evocative concept that can spark imaginative narratives across genres, from epic space operas to gritty conspiracies, exploring themes of exploration, innovation, survival, and the quest for knowledge in a vast and mysterious universe.

Red Cell Team

A "Red Cell Team" typically refers to a specialized group within an organization that is tasked with conducting simulated attacks or security assessments to test vulnerabilities, identify weaknesses, and enhance *preparedness. This concept is often used in the military, intelligence agencies, cybersecurity firms, and other high-security organizations to assess their defenses and response capabilities in the face of potential threats.*

In fictional storytelling, a "Red Cell Team" can be a compelling element to explore themes of intrigue, strategy, and high-stakes challenges. Here are some ways this concept could be incorporated into a story:

1. **Espionage Thriller**: *The story could revolve around a covert Red Cell Team operating in the shadows to infiltrate rival intelligence agencies, corporate headquarters, or government facilities. As the team executes intricate simulations and tests, they uncover a conspiracy that threatens global security, leading to a complex web of deception, betrayal, and espionage.*

2. **Heist Adventure**: *In a high-octane caper narrative, a Red Cell Team could be hired to orchestrate a simulated heist on a museum, bank, or high-security facility to test the defenses and vulnerabilities of the target. The story unfolds as the team navigates intricate security measures, outwits rival criminals, and races against time to pull off the ultimate simulation.*

3. **Cybersecurity Drama**: *Set in the world of digital warfare and cyber espionage, the story could follow a Red Cell Team tasked with conducting simulated cyber-attacks on critical infrastructure, government networks, or corporate systems to test their resilience against virtual threats. As the team delves into the dark web, decodes encrypted messages, and engages in virtual combat, they uncover a cyber conspiracy with far-reaching consequences.*

4. **Survival Challenge**: *In a post-apocalyptic setting, a Red Cell Team could be part of a survival experiment where individuals are tasked with*

testing their skills, resourcefulness, and teamwork in extreme conditions. The story could explore themes of resilience, ingenuity, and the human spirit as the team faces harsh environments, deadly challenges, and moral dilemmas to prove their worth in a world turned upside down.

Whether set in the world of espionage, cyber warfare, heists, or survival challenges, a "Red Cell Team" offers a dynamic narrative device to explore themes of strategy, teamwork, risk-taking, and the ever-evolving nature of security and defense in a complex and unpredictable world.

ABOUT THE K-REPORT

When you want to address an idea like constructing a report that combines a written section with a generated part, you have to call it something. It seemed as though then word *Report* is ok, but what kind of report. So, *K* seemed appropriate as it has been used before in Service Science, in the form of *k-Factor* that is the ratio of intangible service over tangible service in the form:

k-Factor = (intangible service)/(tangible service)

Secondly, how is generated text represented? The query is an underlined bold face sentence and the result generated by GhatGTP is printed as a italics lines of text as in:

ChatGTP

ChatGPT is a branch of AI language models developed by OpenAI that uses generative technology to generate human-like text conversation. ChatGPT leverages the power of the GPT (Generative Pre-trained Transformer) architecture, which is a type of deep learning model trained on vast amounts of text data to understand and generate human language.

ChatGPT models are designed to engage in open-ended conversations with users, responding to text inputs in a conversational manner. These AI models can understand context, generate relevant responses, and maintain coherence throughout a dialogue, making them effective in chatbot applications, language understanding tasks, and virtual assistant interactions.

The advancements in ChatGPT models have enabled more natural and contextually appropriate responses in conversational AI systems, enhancing user experiences and interactions with intelligent virtual agents. ChatGPT models are continually being improved and fine-tuned to deliver more accurate, relevant, and engaging conversations across various domains and languages.

And that is it?

INDEX

ABOUT THE AUTHOR

Harry Katzan, Jr. is an AI consultant specializing in deep learning and neural networks. He was formerly a professor, department chairman, and computer consultant. He has worked for Boeing, Oak Ridge National Laboratory, and IBM. He is the author of 89 books, of which 29 are on computers, and an equal number of peer-reviewed papers. He and his wife have lived in Switzerland where he was a banking consultant and a visiting professor. He is an avid runner and has completed 94 marathons including Boston 13 times and New York 14 times. He holds bachelors, masters, and doctorate degrees.. He is an experienced designer and programmer, and has worked 2 years on a LISP project and another two years on a Prolog project.

Printed in the United States
by Baker & Taylor Publisher Services